PRACTICE

REALITY TRANSURFING

Guided Visualizations to Shift You into Your Dream Life

The Mirror Technique

JOHN K. BELL

DEDICATION & THANKS

I would like to dedicate this piece of work to the human race. You have a special window of opportunity right now to transcend all your challenges.

A special thanks to my family. Thank you for your support. This is for you!

Copyright © 2024 John K. Bell

All rights reserved.

CONTENTS

Dedication & Thanks 1
Forward 3
How to use the Guided Visualizations in the Book 8
The Mirror Technique Guided Visualizations 10
    1. Creating Personal Discipline in Your Life 11
    2. Building Unshakable Confidence 16
    3. Manifesting Your Ideal Weight 22
    4. Creating Authentic Relationships 27
    5. Cultivating Academic Excellence 32
    Review Request 37
    6. Enhancing Artistic Creativity 38
    7. Manifesting Physical Fitness 44
    8. Developing the Confidence of an Articulate Public Speaker ... 49
    9. Getting Rid of Stress 53
    10. Overcoming Fears 57
    11. Cultivating Mindfulness 61
    12. Creating Your Dream Career 65
    13. Manifesting Spiritual Growth 71
    14. Creating Joyful Living 76
    15. Manifesting Perfect Health 81
    16. Cultivating Freedom 85
    17. Manifesting a Life of Ease and Flow 90
    18. Manifesting Miracles and Synchronicities 95
    19. Discovering Your Life Purpose 100
    20. Achieving a State of Emotional Mastery and Resilience 105
    21. Achieving a State of Optimal Mental Clarity 110
Afterthought 115

FORWARD

If you're reading this book, chances are you've heard about the incredible power of Reality Transurfing and are eager to learn how to harness it to transform your life. Congratulations on taking this first step towards manifesting your dreams!

Reality Transurfing, a teaching introduced by the Russian Quantum Physicist, Vadim Zeland, asserts that our reality is not a fixed or immutable entity. Rather, it is a malleable reflection of our thoughts, beliefs, and expectations. Just like a mirror reflects the image placed before it, our reality reflects the content of our minds. By consciously choosing our thoughts and attitudes, we have the power to shape our lives in profound ways.

At the heart of Reality Transurfing lies the concept of the Alternatives Space, a vast realm of infinite possibilities where every conceivable version of reality exists. This space contains all potential scenarios, events, and outcomes, waiting to be manifested into our physical reality based on our thoughts, emotions, and beliefs.

The Mirror Technique, which is the focus of this book, is a powerful tool for navigating the Alternatives Space and manifesting the reality we desire. Through a series of guided visualizations, you'll learn how to effectively use this technique to address specific issues and manifest favorable outcomes in various areas of your life.

Many of us go through life feeling like helpless victims of circumstance, believing that our reality is something that happens to us, rather than something we create. We may find ourselves constantly struggling against the reflection in the mirror, trying in vain to change what we don't like. But the key to true transformation lies not in battling external reality, but in changing the internal images, thoughts, and beliefs that we hold.

The concept of reality as a mirror may seem simple, but its implications are profound. It means that every experience we have, every person we meet, and every circumstance we encounter is a reflection of our inner world. If we don't like what we see in our lives, we have the power to change it by changing ourselves and choosing a different path in the Alternatives Space.

This idea can be both empowering and challenging. On one hand, it puts the responsibility for our lives squarely in our own hands. We can no longer blame others or external circumstances for our problems or limitations. On the other hand, it can be difficult to face the fact that we have created our current reality, especially if it's not what we want.

But the good news is that just as we have created our current reality, we have the power to create a new one. By learning to use the Mirror Technique in conjunction with an understanding of the Alternatives Space, we can begin to consciously shape our thoughts, beliefs, and expectations to align with the life we truly desire.

5 | PRACTICE REALITY TRANSURFING

The Mirror Technique involves visualizing our desired reality as if it were already a present fact, while simultaneously understanding that this desired reality exists as a potential in the Alternatives Space. By engaging all of our senses and emotions in the visualization process, we create a vivid, compelling image that our subconscious mind accepts as real. As we continue to focus on this image, we begin to navigate the Alternatives Space towards the reality we have envisioned.

This process works because our subconscious mind does not distinguish between what is "real" and what is vividly imagined. When we feed it images of success, abundance, joy, and fulfillment, it goes to work creating circumstances that match those images. It's like setting a destination in the vast expanse of the Alternatives Space. With proper focus and intention, we will naturally move towards that chosen reality.

Of course, using the Mirror Technique is not about sitting back and waiting for miracles to happen. It's about taking inspired action towards our goals, while maintaining an unwavering faith in the Universe's ability to support us. As we align our thoughts, beliefs, and actions with our desired reality, we begin to see evidence of it showing up in our lives.

One of the most powerful aspects of the Mirror Technique is its ability to help us overcome limiting beliefs and negative thought patterns. Many of us have unconscious beliefs that hold us back from achieving our full potential. We may believe that we're not good enough, smart enough, or deserving enough to have what we truly want.

By using the Mirror Technique to visualize ourselves as already possessing the qualities and circumstances we desire, we begin to break down these limiting beliefs. We start to see ourselves in a new light - as capable, worthy, and deserving of our dreams. As we continue to reinforce this new self-image, our beliefs begin to shift, and we start to navigate the Alternatives Space towards realities that reflect our expanded sense of possibility.

Another key aspect of the Mirror Technique is the practice of gratitude. When we focus on what we're grateful for in our current reality, we attract more of those positive experiences and circumstances into our lives. Gratitude shifts our focus from lack and limitation to abundance and possibility. It opens us up to receive even more blessings and opportunities, and it aligns us with the realities in the Alternatives Space that are most fulfilling and joyful.

In the guided visualizations that follow, you'll have the opportunity to practice gratitude as part of the Mirror Technique. You'll learn how to cultivate a deep sense of appreciation for all the good that's already present in your life, while also envisioning even greater blessings to come.

As you work with the Mirror Technique and navigate the Alternatives Space, it's important to approach the process with an open mind and a willingness to let go of attachment to specific outcomes. While it's essential to have clear goals and intentions, we must also trust in the Universe's wisdom and timing. Sometimes what we think we want isn't actually what's best for us, or there may be a more efficient path to our goals than we can currently see.

By staying open to possibilities and surrendering to the flow of life, we allow the Universe to guide us through the Alternatives Space in ways that we may never have imagined. We may find that our dreams manifest in ways that are even better than we had originally envisioned, or that new opportunities arise that we hadn't even considered.

7 | PRACTICE REALITY TRANSURFING

Another important aspect of working with the Mirror Technique is consistency. Just like any new skill or habit, the more we practice, the more proficient we become at navigating the Alternatives Space and manifesting our desired realities. It's recommended that you work with the guided visualizations in this book on a daily basis, ideally at the same time each day. This helps to train your mind to focus on your desired reality and reinforces the positive images and beliefs you're cultivating.

It's also important to approach the practice with patience and self-compassion. Manifesting our dreams may take time, and there may be setbacks and challenges along the way. It's essential to maintain a positive attitude and to trust in the process, even when things don't seem to be going as planned.

Remember, every challenge is an opportunity for growth and learning. By staying committed to your vision and continuing to work with the Mirror Technique, you'll develop the mental and emotional resilience needed to weather any storm and emerge victorious.

As you embark on this journey of self-discovery and transformation, know that you are not alone. Countless others have used the Mirror Technique to manifest incredible changes in their lives, and you can too. By connecting with a community of like-minded individuals who are also practicing Reality Transurfing, you can gain support, inspiration, and encouragement along the way.

In the following chapters, you'll find a series of guided visualizations designed to help you address specific issues and manifest your desired outcomes. Each visualization is accompanied by detailed instructions and explanations, so you can fully understand and apply the principles of the Mirror

Technique and navigate the Alternatives Space with confidence.

Whether you're seeking to improve your relationships, enhance your career, increase your abundance, or simply create a more joyful and fulfilling life, the Mirror Technique and the Alternatives Space hold the key to your success. By harnessing the power of your mind and aligning your thoughts, beliefs, and actions with your dreams, you'll be amazed at how quickly and easily your reality begins to shift.

So, take a deep breath, relax, and get ready to embark on the adventure of a lifetime. Your dreams are waiting for you, and the Mirror Technique is your compass for navigating the vast expanse of the Alternatives Space. Let's get started on this transformative journey together!

HOW TO USE THE GUIDED VISUALIZATIONS IN THE BOOK

To get the most out of the guided visualizations in this book, find a quiet, comfortable space where you can relax without interruptions. You may want to use meditation music to help create a peaceful atmosphere and enhance your focus. Many people find that soft, instrumental music without lyrics works best.

Before beginning each visualization, take a few deep breaths and allow yourself to settle into a calm, receptive state. Then, either read through the visualization slowly and carefully, or listen to a recording of the visualization. If you prefer to listen, you have two options:

1. Record yourself reading the visualization in your own voice. This can be especially effective, as your subconscious mind will respond well to the familiarity

and comfort of your own voice. Speak slowly, clearly, and with feeling, allowing yourself to fully engage with the words and images.

2. Purchase the audio version of the book, which includes professional recordings of all the guided visualizations. This can be a convenient option if you don't want to record the visualizations yourself, or if you find that you respond well to the narrator's voice.

Whichever option you choose, close your eyes and immerse yourself in the words and images of the visualization. Use all of your senses to make the experience as vivid and real as possible. Allow yourself to feel the emotions associated with your desired reality, and trust that by aligning your thoughts and beliefs with this vision, you are navigating the Alternatives Space towards its manifestation.

After each visualization, take a few moments to reflect on your experience. Notice any insights, inspirations, or shifts in your energy or perspective. Remember, consistency is key, so make a commitment to practice the visualizations regularly, ideally at the same time each day.

By engaging fully with these guided visualizations, whether through your own recordings or the audio version of the book, you'll harness the power of the Mirror Technique to transform your life and manifest your intention.

THE MIRROR TECHNIQUE GUIDED VISUALIZATIONS

1. Creating Personal Discipline in Your Life

Welcome to this transformative visualization experience, where we will harness the power of personal discipline through the lens of Reality Transurfing. Reality Transurfing is a profound philosophy that empowers you to consciously shape your reality by aligning your thoughts, emotions, and actions with your desired outcomes. By mastering the principles of Reality Transurfing, you can cultivate a life of purpose, fulfillment, and unwavering discipline.

To begin, find a quiet and comfortable space where you can sit or lie down without distractions. Close your eyes and take a few deep, slow breaths. With each inhale, feel your body filling with calming energy, and with each exhale, release any tension or stress that you may be holding onto. Allow yourself to sink into a state of deep relaxation, letting go of any worries or concerns. Feel your muscles loosening, your mind quieting, and your entire being surrendering to the present moment. The Principle of Relaxation in Reality Transurfing reminds us that by releasing resistance and embracing inner peace, we open ourselves up to the limitless possibilities that await us.

As you rest in this relaxed state, bring your attention to your intentions for this visualization. What aspects of personal discipline do you wish to cultivate in your life? Perhaps you desire to develop a stronger sense of commitment to your goals, or maybe you want to enhance your ability to focus and stay motivated in the face of challenges. Whatever your specific intentions may be, visualize them clearly in your mind's eye. See yourself embodying these qualities, and feel the power of your intentions radiating from your core. The Principle of Intention emphasizes that our focused intentions have the power to shape our reality and guide us toward our desired outcomes.

Now, allow your imagination to take flight as you enter a vivid visualization. Picture yourself standing in a serene, orderly space that represents the epitome of discipline and structure. This could be a pristine office, a minimalist living room, or any environment that embodies the qualities you wish to cultivate. As you explore this space, notice the attention to detail, the purposeful arrangement of objects, and the overall sense of harmony and efficiency.

As you continue to observe your surroundings, a stunning mirror catches your eye. You approach the mirror and gaze into its reflection, and what you see takes your breath away. In the mirror, you behold a version of yourself that exudes discipline, determination, and unwavering focus. Your posture is tall and confident, your eyes are clear and purposeful, and your entire being radiates an aura of self-mastery.

As you continue to gaze into the mirror, you realize that this reflection is not just an image, but a powerful metaphor for the reality you are creating. The Principle of the Mirror in Reality Transurfing suggests that our outer world is a direct reflection of our inner state. Just as the mirror reflects your disciplined self, your thoughts, beliefs, and attitudes shape the reality you experience.

With this understanding, you begin to consciously align your thoughts and emotions with the disciplined version of yourself in the mirror. You affirm to yourself, "I am disciplined, focused, and committed to my goals." Again, "I am disciplined, focused, and committed to my goals." As you repeat this affirmation, you notice the reflection in the mirror becoming clearer, more vibrant, and more alive. You feel a surge of energy and motivation flowing through you, empowering you to embody the qualities of discipline in every aspect of your life.

13 | PRACTICE REALITY TRANSURFING

As you bask in the presence of your disciplined reflection, you may notice thoughts or doubts arising, attempting to pull you away from your vision. These may be old limiting beliefs, fears of failure, or any other mental obstacles that have held you back in the past. Acknowledge these thoughts without judgment, and then gently release them. Imagine these limiting beliefs as weights that you have been carrying, and now, with each exhale, you are letting them go, one by one. Feel the lightness and freedom that comes with releasing these burdens, making space for a reality of discipline and purpose. The Principle of Letting Go reminds us that by detaching from specific outcomes and trusting in the natural flow of the universe, we allow our desired reality to manifest with greater ease and grace.

With your limiting beliefs released, you now find yourself connecting with the Alternatives Space, a realm of infinite possibilities and potential. This is the space where all realities exist simultaneously, waiting for you to choose and align with the one that best serves your intentions. In your mind's eye, see yourself stepping into a version of reality where discipline is your natural state of being. In this space, you effortlessly make choices that support your goals, you maintain unwavering focus, and you embrace challenges as opportunities for growth. Feel the energy of this Alternative Space flowing through you, filling you with the confidence and determination to manifest your disciplined self in your everyday life. The Principle of the Alternatives Space in Reality Transurfing reminds you that by consciously choosing and aligning with the reality you desire, you have the power to shape your experiences.

As you continue to align with the Alternatives Space, take a moment to assess your energy and emotions. Are there any lingering negative thoughts or feelings that may be blocking your path to discipline? If so, acknowledge them and consciously choose to replace them with positive, empowering beliefs. Visualize a warm, golden light emanating from your heart center, filling your entire being with the energy of discipline, focus, and determination. Feel this light growing brighter and stronger with each breath, purifying any remaining negativity and infusing you with the strength to persevere. Affirm to yourself, "I am filled with the energy of discipline. I have the power to shape my reality through my thoughts, emotions, and actions."

In this elevated state of awareness, take a moment to express gratitude for the abundance and opportunities that are already present in your life. Acknowledge the progress you have made, the lessons you have learned, and the people who have supported you along the way. Feel a deep sense of appreciation for the journey itself, knowing that every step, every challenge, and every victory has contributed to the person you are becoming. As you cultivate this attitude of gratitude, you align yourself with the flow of abundance and attract even more positive experiences into your reality. The Principle of Gratitude teaches us that by focusing on what we appreciate, we open ourselves up to receiving more of what we desire.

As you prepare to conclude this visualization, take a few deep breaths and allow the insights and experiences you have gained to integrate into your being. Feel the transformation that has taken place within you, the newfound sense of discipline, clarity, and purpose that now resides in your core. Visualize yourself carrying this energy of discipline into your daily life, making choices and taking actions that align with your highest intentions. See yourself effortlessly maintaining focus, staying committed to your goals, and embracing challenges with resilience and determination. Trust that the universe is conspiring in your favor, guiding you towards your envisioned reality.

15 | PRACTICE REALITY TRANSURFING

As you gently return your awareness to the present moment, take a final deep breath and open your eyes. Feel the ground beneath you, the air around you, and the life force flowing through you. Know that you have the power to shape your reality through your thoughts, emotions, and actions. The discipline and determination you have cultivated during this visualization are now a part of you, guiding you towards a life of purpose and fulfillment.

Carry this energy of discipline with you as you navigate your day, remembering that every choice you make is an opportunity to align with your highest potential. Trust in the principles of Reality Transurfing, and know that the universe is always supporting you in manifesting your desired reality.

Thank you for dedicating this time to your personal growth and transformation. May you continue to embrace discipline, focus, and determination in all that you do, and may your journey be filled with abundance, joy, and endless possibilities. As you step forward into your day or sleep, remember to carry a heart full of gratitude, knowing that the universe is conspiring in your favor always.

2. Building Unshakable Confidence

Welcome to this guided visualization for boosting confidence through the principles of Reality Transurfing. Before we begin, take a moment to set a clear intention for this practice. Affirm to yourself, "I am here to cultivate unwavering self-assurance and trust in my ability to shape my reality."

Reality Transurfing teaches us that our thoughts and beliefs create our experiences, and by aligning our inner state with our desired outcomes, we can manifest the confidence we seek. This is the Principle of Intention – by focusing our minds on what we want to experience, we set the stage for its manifestation.

Find a comfortable position, either seated with a straight spine or lying down with your arms and legs uncrossed. Close your eyes and take a few deep breaths, inhaling slowly through your nose and exhaling gently through your mouth. With each exhalation, allow any tension or stress to melt away, as if you're releasing it into the earth below. Feel your body growing heavier, sinking into your seat or mat, completely supported and at ease.

As you continue to breathe slowly and deeply, notice your mind becoming calm, like a still lake on a windless day.

Now, bring your attention to your intentions for this visualization. Ask yourself, "What does confidence mean to me? How do I want to feel and act in situations that challenge my self-assurance?" Maybe you envision yourself speaking up in meetings, asserting your ideas with clarity and conviction. Or perhaps you see yourself navigating social situations with ease, engaging in conversations and forming connections effortlessly. Take a few moments to clarify your desires and intentions, knowing that the clearer you are, the more effectively you can align with your desired reality. This is the Principle of Clarity; the more specific and vivid our intentions, the more powerfully they can manifest.

17 | PRACTICE REALITY TRANSURFING

As you hold these intentions in your mind, imagine yourself transported to a serene, beautiful space. You find yourself standing in front of a towering, ornate mirror, its golden frame glinting in soft, ethereal light. As you gaze into the mirror, you see your reflection – but instead of your current self-image, you're greeted by an ultra-confident version of yourself.

Notice how you stand tall and proud, your shoulders back and your head held high. Your posture exudes self-assurance and poise. Your eyes sparkle with a deep inner knowing, a trust in your abilities and your path. Your smile radiates warmth and authenticity, drawing others in with its magnetic charm.

As you observe this confident version of yourself, remember that the world around you is a mirror, reflecting your thoughts, beliefs, and attitudes. Just as you see a self-assured, empowered version of yourself in the mirror, know that by embodying these qualities within, you will begin to see them reflected in your outer reality.

Now, watch as this confident version of you begins to interact with the world around you. Notice how people respond to your self-assured energy, treating you with respect and admiration. Observe how doors open for you, opportunities arise, and challenges melt away in the face of your unwavering confidence.

See the world around you shimmering and shifting, transforming to match your inner state of self-assurance. Witness your relationships deepening, your career flourishing, and your dreams manifesting with ease and grace. The more you embody the energy of confidence, the more your outer reality aligns to reflect this inner state.

Allow yourself to fully embrace this experience, knowing that by holding the vision of your confident self and the world that reflects it, you are powerfully influencing your reality. Feel the energy of self-assurance emanating from your being, rippling out into the world around you, and drawing forth experiences and circumstances that match your newfound confidence.

Take a few moments to fully immerse yourself in this vision, feeling the profound connection between your inner state and your outer reality. Know that by nurturing confidence within, you are not only transforming your self-image but also shaping the world around you, creating a life that mirrors your deepest desires and grandest visions.

As you savor this experience, imagine a radiant light emanating from your confident self, filling the mirror and spilling out into the world around you. This light represents the power of your intention, the clarity of your vision, and the unwavering faith in your ability to manifest your desires.

When you feel ready, take a deep breath and gently release your connection to the mirror, knowing that you carry this confidence with you wherever you go. The mirror dissolves, but the energy of self-assurance remains, forever imprinted on your being and reflected in the world around you.

As you immerse yourself in this experience of confidence, release any attachment to specific outcomes or limitations. Let go of the 'how' and trust that by aligning your inner state with your intentions, your outer reality will naturally shift in the most harmonious way. Surrender control and allow the Universe to orchestrate the details, knowing that your job is simply to embody the confidence you wish to experience. This is the Principle of Letting Go, as we release our grip on 'how' things should unfold, we open ourselves to unexpected opportunities and synchronicities.

19 | PRACTICE REALITY TRANSURFING

In Reality Transurfing, there exists a realm known as the Alternatives Space – an infinite field of potentiality where all possible versions of reality exist. In this space, there are versions of you living your ideal life, embodying your deepest desires and grandest visions. Connect with this space now, and feel yourself aligning with the version of reality where your confidence is unbreakable, and your world reflects this inner state. Know that this reality is not separate from you – it is available to you at every moment. By focusing your energy and attention on it, you draw it closer, collapsing the quantum wave of potential into your lived experience.

As you align with this confident reality, take a moment to scan your energy field for any negative or limiting beliefs that may be blocking your self-assurance. Maybe there are old stories or self-doubts that have been holding you back, whispering that you're not good enough or that you'll never succeed. Acknowledge these beliefs without judgment, and then imagine them dissolving like mist in the morning sun, replaced by empowering thoughts and emotions. Feel a balanced, harmonious energy flowing through you, confidence permeating every cell of your being.

Steeped in this energy of confidence, cultivate a deep sense of gratitude and appreciation for your ability to shape your reality. Thank yourself for showing up for this visualization, for having the courage and commitment to embrace your most confident self. Feel gratitude for all the challenges and experiences that have shaped you, knowing that they have served to strengthen your resilience and self-trust.

Begin to integrate this experience into your being, knowing that you can access this state of confidence whenever you need it. Imagine this feeling of self-assurance anchoring into your cells, into your subconscious mind, becoming your new default state. Know that the more you practice embodying confidence, the more naturally it will arise in your daily life, and the more your world will reflect this inner transformation. You are reprogramming your self-image, becoming the confident creator of your reality.

As you prepare to return to your waking life, take a deep breath and feel your body once again, wiggling your fingers and toes. Gently blink your eyes open, gazing softly ahead. Carry this feeling of empowerment with you as you move through your day, knowing that your outer reality is a reflection of your inner state. Remember, your thoughts and beliefs shape your experiences. By choosing to focus on confidence and self-assurance, you become the master of your reality, able to surf the waves of life with grace and ease.

Know that this confidence is not something you need to strive for or attain – it is your birthright, your natural state of being. Trust in your innate wisdom and ability to navigate life's challenges, remembering that every experience is an opportunity to strengthen your self-assurance. You are a powerful creator, and your reality molds itself around your beliefs.

Carry this knowing with you as you move forward, and trust that the Universe is conspiring in your favor, bringing you the experiences and opportunities that align with your highest intentions. Stay open to the magic and miracles that await, and embrace your journey with a deep trust in yourself and in the unfolding of your path.

Take a final deep breath, and when you're ready, fully open your eyes, returning to the room around you. Remember, you are the author of your reality, and with each thought and intention, you paint the canvas of your life. Choose your colors wisely, and trust in the masterpiece that is unfolding, knowing that your world is a mirror, reflecting the magnificence and confidence that resides within you.

3. Manifesting Your Ideal Weight

Welcome to this transformative visualization session, where we'll harness the power of Reality Transurfing to align our inner world with our desired outer reality of achieving our ideal weight. Reality Transurfing is a powerful framework that emphasizes the role of our intentions and beliefs in shaping our experiences. By focusing on our end goal and surrendering to the natural flow of the universe, we can manifest the changes we seek with ease and grace. Throughout this visualization, we'll explore the key principles of Reality Transurfing, using them as a guide to reshape our relationship with our bodies and our weight. So, let's embark on this journey together, opening ourselves to the limitless potential within.

To begin, find a quiet space where you can be free from distractions. Settle into a comfortable position, either seated or lying down, and allow your body to relax fully. You can now close your eyes. Take a deep breath in through your nose, filling your lungs with fresh, cleansing air. As you exhale through your mouth, imagine releasing any tensions, worries, or stresses that you may be holding onto. Continue this deep, intentional breathing, letting each inhale infuse your body with a sense of peace and each exhale carry away any residual tightness or resistance. Feel your body becoming heavier, sinking into the surface beneath you as your mind grows quieter and more still. This is your time to simply be, letting go of any demands or expectations and allowing yourself to fully embrace the present moment.

As you rest in this state of deep relaxation, bring your awareness to your intention for this visualization—aligning with your ideal weight. Take a moment to connect with the reasons behind this goal. Perhaps it's to feel more energized and confident, to improve your health, or to live more fully in alignment with your highest self. Whatever your reasons, let them resonate deeply within you, fueling your commitment to this transformative process. Visualize yourself embodying these intentions, radiating the qualities you desire. See yourself as the version of you who has already achieved your ideal weight, feeling the sense of lightness, vitality, and ease that comes with this accomplishment. Allow this vision to fill you with a sense of excitement and possibility, knowing that this reality is within your reach.

Now, let's deepen this vision through a powerful visualization exercise. Imagine yourself standing in front of a full-length mirror, taking in your reflection. But this is no ordinary mirror—it reflects not just your current physical form, but also the infinite potential within you.

In Reality Transurfing, the mirror technique suggests that our outer world is a reflection of our inner state. Just as a mirror reflects back the image we present to it, our reality reflects back our dominant thoughts, beliefs, and attitudes. By changing the "image" we project internally, we can shift the reflection we see externally.

As you gaze into this special mirror, see yourself transform, your body shifting and morphing until you embody your ideal weight. Notice how your posture becomes more upright and your muscles more toned. Observe the radiant glow of your skin and the sparkle in your eyes, reflecting your inner vitality. Feel the lightness and ease with which you move, as if gravity itself has loosened its grip.

Know that as you hold this empowered self-image in your mind, you are projecting it out into the mirror of your world. By focusing on this ideal version of yourself, both in your mind's eye and through your actions and energy, you will begin to see it reflected back to you in your outer reality.

Experience the joy and confidence that comes from inhabiting your ideal body, letting these feelings wash over you and imprint themselves on your subconscious mind. Embrace the understanding that your reality is a reflection of your inner state—and commit to holding the vision and vibration of your healthiest, most aligned self.

As you savor this vision of your ideal self, bring your awareness to any resistance or doubts that may arise. These may manifest as thoughts like "It's too hard to lose weight" or "I've tried before and failed." Acknowledge these thoughts without judgment, understanding that they are simply remnants of old patterns and beliefs.

Now, imagine yourself gently releasing these limiting ideas, watching them drift away like leaves on a stream. In their place, plant the seeds of new, empowering beliefs. Repeat silently to yourself: "My body is a miraculous, self-healing system. I trust in its wisdom and its ability to find its natural balance. I release the need to control or force change, and instead, I allow my ideal weight to manifest with ease and grace." Feel these affirmations taking root within you, reshaping your inner landscape.

In Reality Transurfing, we learn of the Alternatives Space, this a realm of infinite possibilities where all variations of reality exist simultaneously. It is from this space that we draw the raw materials to shape our experiences. So, let's connect with this boundless reservoir now. Imagine a vast, luminous space stretching out before you, pulsating with pure potential. Within this space, locate the version of reality where you have already achieved your ideal weight. It may appear as a glowing orb or a shimmering portal. Approach this beacon of possibility and allow yourself to merge with it, feeling the energy of your desired outcome flowing through every cell of your being. Affirm silently: "I am now aligned with the reality of my ideal weight. This is my truth, and I welcome it into my life with open arms." Feel the power of this alignment, knowing that you are now a magnet for the people, resources, and opportunities that will support your transformation.

As you bask in the energy of your desired reality, take a moment to check in with your own energetic state. Are you radiating the vibration of health, vitality, and self-love? Or are there any lingering traces of self-doubt, frustration, or negativity? If you notice any discordant energies, imagine them as dense, heavy clouds within your body. Now, visualize a brilliant light emanating from your heart center, growing brighter and more expansive with each breath. Let this light fill your entire being, dissolving any clouds of negativity and replacing them with the pure, radiant energy of love and acceptance. Affirm: "I am a being of light, radiating health and positivity. I release any patterns of self-sabotage or negative self-talk, and I choose to nourish myself with kindness, compassion, and respect." Feel your energy shifting, coming into harmony with your highest intentions.

As you continue to bathe in the light of your own loving presence, let a profound sense of gratitude wash over you. Give thanks for the miraculous body that is your home in this life, recognizing all the ways it supports and sustains you every day. Extend your appreciation to the journey of growth and self-discovery you are on, knowing that each step, each challenge, is an opportunity to evolve and expand. Acknowledge the abundance of resources and support that surround you, from the nourishing food that fuels your body to the loving relationships that feed your soul. Allow this gratitude to fill you up from the inside out, overflowing into every aspect of your life. Silently affirm: "I am deeply grateful for my body, my life, and all the blessings that flow to me. I trust in the wisdom of the universe and the perfection of my journey." Feel the magnetic power of gratitude, knowing that it aligns you with the flow of abundance and miracles.

As we prepare to bring this visualization to a close, take a moment to reflect on the shifts and insights you've experienced. What new perspectives have emerged? What old patterns have you released? What empowering truths have you claimed? Allow these realizations to crystallize within you, forming a clear, unwavering intention for the path ahead. Silently affirm: "I now integrate the lessons and blessings of this visualization into my life. I carry forward the energy of my ideal self, letting it guide my choices and actions. I trust in my ability to manifest my ideal weight, and I embrace the journey with joy and ease." Feel these words resonating through your being, etching themselves into the fabric of your reality. Know that you are the creator of your experience, and that by aligning your energy and intentions, you have the power to shape your world.

As you slowly begin to return your awareness to the present moment, you can carry with you the peace, clarity, and empowerment you've cultivated. Know that the seeds you've planted in your consciousness will continue to grow and blossom, even when you're not actively focused on them. Trust in the unfolding of your journey, remembering that the universe is always conspiring in your favor. Take a deep breath in, savoring the sweetness of this moment. As you exhale, gently wiggle your fingers and toes, feeling your connection to the physical world. When you're ready, slowly open your eyes, allowing yourself to adjust to the light. Carry this newfound radiance with you as you move through your day, letting it illuminate every interaction and experience. And always remember: you are a powerful creator, capable of shaping your reality with the force of your intentions and beliefs. Step into your power, and watch as your world transforms to match your most luminous vision.

4. Creating Authentic Relationships

Welcome to this transformative journey of enhancing your relationships through the power of Reality Transurfing. As we embark on this visualization, take a moment to set a clear intention for the connections you wish to cultivate. Perhaps you desire more understanding, compassion, or deeper bonds with your loved ones. Whatever your intention may be, hold it close to your heart and trust that through the principles of Reality Transurfing, you have the power to shape your reality and manifest the relationships you truly desire. Reality Transurfing teaches us that our outer world is a reflection of our inner state, and by consciously aligning our thoughts, beliefs, and actions with our goals, we become the architects of our own experiences.

Find a quiet space where you can be free from distractions and allow yourself to fully relax. Settle into a comfortable position, whether seated or lying down, and begin to bring your attention to your breath. Gently close your eyes as you inhale deeply, filling your lungs with fresh, cleansing air, and exhale slowly, releasing any tension or stress that you may be holding in your body. With each breath, feel yourself sinking deeper into a state of relaxation, letting go of any worries or thoughts that may be weighing on your mind. Allow your breath to be your anchor, guiding you into a profound state of peace and tranquility. As you continue to breathe deeply, notice how your body becomes heavier, melting into the surface beneath you. Feel the gentle rise and fall of your chest, the rhythmic flow of air in and out of your nostrils, and the gradual quieting of your mind. In this state of deep relaxation, you become more receptive to the transformative power of this visualization.

Now, bring your focus to your intentions for your relationships. Take a moment to visualize the kind of connections you long to create. Perhaps you envision relationships filled with open communication, where both parties feel heard and understood. Maybe you desire interactions overflowing with laughter, joy, and shared moments of happiness. Or perhaps you seek a deep sense of trust, where you can be your authentic self without fear of judgment. Allow yourself to explore what truly matters to you in your relationships. As you hold these intentions in your mind, feel the alignment between your desires and your highest truth. Affirm to yourself, "I am open to giving and receiving love in all my relationships. I attract connections that nourish my soul and help me grow." Feel the power of your words resonating through every cell of your being, anchoring your intentions into your reality.

As you continue to hold your intentions, imagine yourself transported to a beautiful, tranquil space. This could be a lush garden filled with fragrant flowers, a serene beach with gentle waves lapping at the shore, or any other location that evokes a sense of peace and harmony within you. In this sacred space, you encounter a large, gilded mirror. As you approach the mirror, you see your reflection transforming into your highest, most loving self. You radiate an energy of pure love, compassion, and understanding. The mirror reflects back to you the ideal version of your relationships, filled with joy, connection, and harmony.

Visualize your loved ones appearing in the mirror, one by one. As each person emerges, witness the expressions of love, laughter, and deep connection on their faces. Observe the effortless flow of communication, the genuine understanding, and the heartfelt appreciation that permeates every interaction. The mirror reflects back to you the relationships you desire, showing you that what you see is a reflection of your own thoughts, beliefs, and energy.

Allow yourself to fully immerse in this vision, engaging all your senses. Notice the vivid colors, the gentle sounds, the comforting textures, and the loving energy that surrounds you.

The more vividly you experience this visualization, the more deeply it becomes imprinted in your subconscious mind, paving the way for its manifestation in your reality. Remember, the mirror is a powerful tool, reflecting back to you the quality of your inner world. As you focus on love, connection, and harmony, the mirror will continue to reflect those qualities in your relationships.

As you bask in the beauty of your visualized relationships, take a moment to release any attachment to specific outcomes or timelines. Recognize that the universe has its own divine plan and that your role is to align yourself with the flow of life, trusting that everything is unfolding in perfect timing. Surrender any need to control or force situations, and instead, embrace a deep sense of faith in the journey. Trust that as you continue to vibrate at the frequency of love and alignment, your relationships will naturally reflect that energy back to you. Release any resistance or doubt, knowing that the more you let go, the more space you create for miracles to occur.

In this state of surrender, allow yourself to connect with the Alternatives Space, the realm of infinite possibilities that exists beyond the limitations of your current reality. In this space, you have access to the version of reality where your desired relationships already exist. Feel yourself merging with the energy of this Alternatives Space, where love, harmony, and deep connection are the natural order. Allow the wisdom of your heart to guide you, trusting that you are always being supported and directed towards your highest good. In this space, there are no obstacles or barriers, only endless potential for growth and transformation. Embrace the knowing that as you align with what is stored in the Alternatives Space, your relationships in the physical world will begin to mirror the love and connection you experience here.

As you continue to bask in the energy of the Alternatives Space, take a moment to check in with your own energy and emotions. Notice any areas where you may be holding onto negative beliefs or patterns that are blocking the flow of love in your relationships. Perhaps there are old wounds or fears that need to be acknowledged and released. Take a deep breath and imagine these limiting beliefs being gently dissolved by the light of your awareness. As you exhale, feel them leaving your body and dissipating into the ether. Replace these old patterns with empowering beliefs such as, "I am worthy of deeply fulfilling relationships," "I attract partners who cherish and support me," and "I am capable of creating the connections I desire." Feel your energy shifting, becoming lighter, clearer, and more aligned with your highest truth.

In this space of clarity and alignment, allow a profound sense of gratitude to wash over you. Give thanks for the loving relationships that already bless your life, and for the new connections that are on their way to you. Recognize that every person in your life, whether past, present, or future, has been a teacher and a catalyst for your growth. Appreciate the lessons you've learned, the love you've shared, and the moments of joy and laughter that have illuminated your path. Gratitude is a powerful magnet, attracting more of what you appreciate into your life. As you focus on the blessings in your relationships, you will find more reasons you'll find to be grateful.

As you prepare to return to your waking reality, take a moment to integrate the insights and experiences you've had during this visualization. Allow the feelings of love, connection, and empowerment to anchor themselves deeply into your being. Know that you have the power to transform your relationships by aligning your thoughts, words, and actions with the truth of who you are. Carry the energy of this visualization with you as you navigate your daily interactions, remembering that you are the creator of your reality. Trust that the seeds you've planted in this sacred space will blossom in perfect timing, bringing you the relationships your heart desires.

Gently begin to bring your awareness back to your physical self, wiggling your fingers and toes, and taking a deep, cleansing breath. Feel the energy of the room around you, the surface beneath you, and the gentle rhythm of your breath. When you're ready, slowly open your eyes, feeling refreshed, centered, and filled with a renewed sense of love and connection. Know that the transformations you've experienced in this visualization are real and lasting, and that you have the power to continue to shape your relationships with every thought, word, and action.

Thank you for dedicating this time to nurturing your relationships and creating a reality filled with love, connection, and understanding. Trust in the journey and have faith that the universe is conspiring in your favor, bringing you the perfect people and experiences to support your growth and happiness. Remember that you are never alone, and that the love you seek is always within you, waiting to be expressed and shared with the world.

5. Cultivating Academic Excellence

Welcome to this transformative visualization session where we will harness the power of Reality Transurfing to cultivate academic excellence. As we embark on this journey together, let us set a clear and purposeful intention to align our academic pursuits with the natural flow of the universe. By doing so, we open ourselves to the infinite possibilities available to us, allowing our desired outcomes to manifest with effortless grace. Reality Transurfing teaches us that our thoughts and beliefs hold the power to shape our reality. By consciously choosing and focusing on our intentions, we become the architects of our own academic success. The Principle of Intention reminds us that our minded focus and unwavering determination have the ability to bring forth the reality we desire.

To begin, find a comfortable position, either seated or lying down, and allow your eyes to gently close. Take a deep, cleansing breath, inhaling peace and exhaling any tensions or worries that may have accumulated throughout your day. As you continue to breathe slowly and deliberately, feel your body sinking into a state of deep relaxation. With each exhale, imagine any remaining stress or tightness melting away, leaving you feeling refreshed and at ease. Embrace this sensation of tranquility, knowing that in this space of inner calm, you are most receptive to the transformative power of this visualization.

Now, bring your attention to the intentions you hold for this visualization and your academic journey as a whole. Take a moment to contemplate what it is you truly wish to achieve. Visualize yourself as the embodiment of academic success, radiating focus, clarity, and unwavering confidence. See yourself absorbing new information with ease, grasping complex concepts with effortless understanding, and retaining knowledge with crystal-clear clarity. Affirm to yourself, "I am the creator of my academic success." Feel the resonance of this statement echoing through every cell of your being, aligning your desires with your intentions. Trust in your innate ability to manifest your chosen reality of academic excellence.

Allow your imagination to transport you to a serene and nurturing study space, a sanctuary designed to support your academic growth and development. As you settle into this space, imagine a large, ornate mirror hanging on the wall before you. Gaze into the mirror and see your reflection radiating with the essence of academic excellence. Notice how your posture exudes confidence and determination, your eyes sparkle with the joy of learning, and your smile reflects the deep satisfaction of achieving your goals. As you continue to observe your reflection, visualize the world around you transforming to mirror your inner state. See the pages of your textbooks coming alive with vibrant understanding, the words leaping off the page and integrating seamlessly into your expanding knowledge base. Witness your tests and assignments marked with the highest grades, reflecting your dedication and mastery of the subject matter. Allow yourself to experience the profound sense of accomplishment and pride that comes with academic success, knowing that your external reality is a direct reflection of your inner beliefs and attitudes. The mirror technique emphasizes the immense power of our minds to shape our experiences, reminding us that by cultivating a positive and focused internal state, we naturally attract corresponding circumstances in our external world.

As you hold this empowering vision in your mind's eye, take a moment to release any attachment to specific outcomes or self-imposed limitations. Acknowledge that the path to your goals may not always unfold in the exact manner you anticipate, and that is okay. Trust in the infinite wisdom of the universe to guide you towards your desired reality in the most harmonious and beneficial way possible. Surrender any need for control, knowing that by aligning your intentions with the natural flow of life, you open yourself to a world of unimaginable possibilities. Embrace the journey of your academic growth, with all its twists and turns, trusting that each step is an essential part of your unique path to success.

Now, let us connect with the transformative concept of the Alternatives Space, a dimension beyond our everyday reality where all potentials exist simultaneously. Imagine yourself tapping into this infinite realm, aligning with the version of reality that fully supports and nurtures your academic aspirations. Feel the boundless energy of this space flowing through you, infusing every cell of your being with the unwavering belief in your ability to achieve greatness. Visualize yourself effortlessly attracting the resources, opportunities, and mentors necessary for your academic success. See doors of possibility swinging open before you, revealing exciting new avenues for learning and growth. Trust that in this Alternatives Space, your intentions are fully supported and manifested with ease and grace. The principle of the Alternatives Space enables us to expand our perception beyond the limitations of our current circumstances, recognizing that we have the power to align with the most favorable outcomes available to us.

As you continue to immerse yourself in this empowering visualization, take a moment to assess your internal state. Notice any negative or limiting beliefs that may be lingering in the depths of your mind, quietly undermining your progress. Acknowledge these thoughts without judgment, understanding that they are simply old patterns that no longer serve you. With a gentle exhale, release these limiting beliefs, watching them drift away like leaves on a gentle breeze. In their place, plant the seeds of positive affirmations and empowering beliefs. Repeat to yourself, "I am capable of achieving my academic dreams. I trust in my innate ability to learn, grow, and excel." Feel the vibrational resonance of these statements infusing every aspect of your being, from the tiniest atom to the vast expanses of your consciousness. Allow these affirmations to take root, blossoming into an unshakable faith in your own potential. By consciously choosing to focus on uplifting thoughts and beliefs, you attract experiences and circumstances that reflect your positive inner state.

As you bask in the glow of your own transformative power, take a moment to cultivate a profound sense of gratitude for the abundance of knowledge and opportunities available to you. Recognize that each challenge you encounter along your academic path is a precious gift, offering you the chance to grow, learn, and expand in ways you never thought possible. Embrace the journey of your education with a heart full of appreciation, knowing that every step, no matter how small, is bringing you closer to the realization of your dreams. Give thanks for the brilliant minds that have come before you, the dedicated teachers who have shared their wisdom, and the supportive community that surrounds you. Allow this gratitude to fill your entire being, radiating outward and attracting even more blessings into your life. As you maintain a constant state of appreciation, you open yourself to the limitless abundance of the universe.

As we prepare to gently release this visualization, take a final moment to integrate the profound insights and transformative experiences you have gained. Acknowledge the shifts in your perspective, the newfound clarity of your intentions, and the unshakable confidence in your ability to manifest academic success. Embrace the feelings of empowerment and alignment, knowing that they will continue to guide and support you long after this visualization has ended. Visualize yourself carrying this radiant energy with you as you navigate your daily life, infusing your studies and interactions with the vibrant essence of your highest potential. Trust in the unwavering support of the universe, knowing that your academic journey is unfolding in perfect harmony with your deepest desires.

As you slowly begin to bring your awareness back to the present moment, take a deep, cleansing breath, feeling the gentle rise and fall of your chest. Wiggle your fingers and toes, gradually reawakening your physical senses. When you feel ready, gently open your eyes, allowing them to adjust to the soft light around you. Carry the peaceful energy and unwavering intention of this visualization with you as you continue on your path to academic excellence. Remember that your dedication to personal growth and your alignment with the principles of Reality Transurfing will continue to manifest profound success in your external reality.

Review Request

Dear Fellow Transurfer,

Thank you for dedicating your time to reading this book. I have a sincere request: please take a moment to visit Amazon and write an honest review about this book. Your review, no matter its length, has the power to inspire others and help spread the transformative principles of Reality Transurfing. By sharing your thoughts, you contribute to the growth of this life-changing philosophy and enable it to reach those who need it most.

With heartfelt gratitude,

J. K. Bell

6. Enhancing Artistic Creativity

Welcome to this transformative visualization experience, designed to help you tap into your limitless potential as an artist and creator. As we embark on this journey together, take a moment to set a clear and heartfelt intention for what you wish to achieve or experience during this session. Whether it's unlocking new levels of creativity, overcoming artistic blocks, or aligning with your highest purpose, trust that your intention will guide you towards the reality you desire. The practice of Reality Transurfing, which forms the foundation of this visualization, suggests that our thoughts, beliefs, and emotions shape our external reality. By mastering our inner world, we gain the power to consciously create our life experiences.

Find a quiet, comfortable space where you can sit or lie down without distractions. Close your eyes and begin to focus on your breath, allowing it to become deep and slow. With each inhale, feel your body filling with calm, soothing energy. And with each exhale, release any tension, stress, or worries that you may be holding onto. As you continue to breathe deeply, notice your body becoming heavier, sinking into the surface beneath you. Feel your muscles relaxing, your mind becoming quiet and still. Allow yourself to fully surrender to this state of deep relaxation, knowing that you are safe, supported, and exactly where you need to be.

In this state of relaxation, bring your attention to your intentions for this visualization. What do you truly desire to create, experience, or embody as an artist? Take a moment to clarify your intentions, making them as specific and vivid as possible. See, feel, and believe in the reality of your intentions, as if they have already come to fruition. Trust that by aligning your thoughts, emotions, and actions with your intentions, you are planting the seeds for their manifestation. The Principle of Intention in Reality Transurfing reminds us that our intentions serve as a beacon, guiding the universe to conspire in our favor and bring forth the opportunities, resources, and synchronicities necessary for their realization.

Now, let your imagination take over as you begin to visualize yourself navigating the reality of your desired artistic experiences. See yourself in your ideal creative space, whether it's a sunlit studio, a vibrant workshop, or a serene natural setting. Engage all of your senses in this visualization, noticing the colors, textures, sounds, and scents that surround you. Feel the tools of your trade in your hands, the brush, the pen, the instrument, or whatever medium you use to bring your art to life. Notice how they feel like an extension of your being, a conduit for your creative energy.

As you begin to work on your art, see yourself in a state of effortless flow, your movements graceful and intuitive. Ideas and inspiration come to you with ease, as if downloaded from a higher source. Witness your creations taking shape before your eyes, each stroke, each line, each note imbued with the essence of your unique artistic vision.

Now, imagine a large, ornate mirror in front of you, reflecting your ideal creative self. See yourself in the mirror, radiating confidence, joy, and artistic mastery. Notice how your thoughts and attitudes about your creativity are reflected back to you in the mirror. If any negative or limiting beliefs arise, consciously replace them with empowering, positive affirmations. Watch as the reflection in the mirror shifts to align with your new, empowered beliefs, reflecting back to you the image of an artist who is capable, inspired, and destined for success. Remember that your external reality is a mirror of your internal state, and by cultivating a mindset of creativity, abundance, and possibility, you attract experiences that match this vibration.

As you continue to immerse yourself in this visualization, bring your awareness to any attachments, expectations, or limitations that may be holding you back from fully embodying your creative potential. These may be fears of failure or judgment, beliefs about what is possible or impossible for you, or a need to control every aspect of your artistic journey. Acknowledge these limitations with compassion, understanding that they have served a purpose in your life, but are no longer needed. Now, imagine yourself gently releasing these limitations, watching them drift away like leaves on a gently flowing river. Feel the lightness and freedom that comes from letting go of what no longer serves you. Trust that by surrendering control and aligning with the natural flow of creativity, you open yourself up to even greater possibilities than your mind can currently conceive. The Principle of Letting Go in Reality Transurfing reminds us that by relinquishing our attachment to specific outcomes, we create space for the universe to bring forth solutions and opportunities beyond our limited perception.

In the Philosophy of Reality Transurfing, there exists a concept known as the Alternatives Space, which is a realm of pure potential, where all possible realities and outcomes exist simultaneously. Imagine yourself now accessing this Alternatives Space, a vast, infinite expanse of swirling energy and possibility. Feel yourself becoming one with this space, your consciousness expanding to merge with its boundless potential. From this space, you have access to all the resources, insights, and inspiration you need to manifest your artistic vision. Visualize your desired artistic reality as a glowing orb of light within this space, pulsating with the energy of its inevitable manifestation. See yourself reaching out and merging with this orb, aligning every cell of your being with the vibrational frequency of your desired reality. Feel the

41 | PRACTICE REALITY TRANSURFING

certainty and inevitability of its manifestation, knowing that it is already done on the level of energy and consciousness.

As you continue to align with your desired artistic reality, take a moment to check in with your inner state. Notice any thoughts, emotions, or sensations that may be arising, without judgment or resistance. If you detect any negative or limiting beliefs, visualize them as dark, heavy clouds within your energy field. Now, imagine a bright, golden light emanating from your heart center, growing brighter and more expansive with each breath. See this light dissolving the clouds of negativity, transmuting them into pure, positive energy. As the light continues to expand, feel it infusing every cell of your being with the vibrations of love, creativity, and abundance. Affirm to yourself: "I am a clear and open channel for creative inspiration. My art flows through me effortlessly and joyfully. I trust in my unique artistic vision and the path of my creative journey."

From this elevated state of energy and alignment, take a moment to cultivate a deep sense of gratitude for your artistic journey and the abundance of creativity that flows through you. Reflect on the challenges and obstacles you have overcome, the lessons you have learned, and the growth you have experienced as an artist. Give thanks for the unique talents, perspectives, and experiences that shape your artistic expression. Feel a profound appreciation for the opportunity to create, to share your gifts with the world, and to make a positive impact through your art. Visualize your art touching the lives of others, inspiring them, uplifting them, and reminding them of the beauty and possibility that exists within and around them. Affirm to yourself: "I am deeply grateful for the endless stream of creativity that flows through me. I appreciate the journey of my artistic evolution, and trust that it is unfolding in perfect timing. I am thankful for the ability to create art that inspires, heals, and transforms."

As you prepare to conclude this visualization, take a moment to integrate the insights, energy, and alignment you have experienced. Visualize yourself moving forward on your artistic path with renewed clarity, confidence, and inspiration. See yourself effortlessly incorporating the principles of Reality Transurfing into your daily life and creative practice, trusting in the power of your intentions, visualizations, and aligned actions to shape your artistic reality. Affirm to yourself: "I am the creator of my artistic journey. I trust in the wisdom of my creative intuition and the guidance of the universe. I am open to receiving the opportunities, resources, and synchronicities that support my artistic growth and success." Know that you can return to this state of aligned creativity whenever you need to, simply by setting your intention and remembering the truth of your creative power.

As we bring this visualization to a close, take a deep, cleansing breath, and gently begin to bring your awareness back to your physical body and surroundings. Wiggle your fingers and toes, feeling the energy of creativity and inspiration circulating through your being. When you are ready, slowly open your eyes, carrying with you the sense of clarity, alignment, and empowerment you have cultivated.

Remember that you are a powerful creator, with the ability to shape your artistic reality through your thoughts, emotions, and actions. Trust in the journey of your creative evolution, and know that the universe is conspiring to support you every step of the way. Take a moment to express gratitude for this experience, and for the boundless creativity that flows through you. As you continue on your artistic path, let the principles of Reality Transurfing guide and inspire you, reminding you of the magic and possibility that exists within and around you.

43 | PRACTICE REALITY TRANSURFING

May your artistic journey be filled with joy, inspiration, and the manifestation of your deepest dreams and desires.

7. Manifesting Physical Fitness

Welcome to this transformative visualization experience, designed to help you harness the incredible power of Reality Transurfing and the Mirror Technique to enhance your physical fitness and overall well-being. As we begin, take a moment to connect with your deepest intentions for this practice. What do you hope to achieve or experience in terms of your health and vitality? Allow these intentions to crystallize clearly in your mind, holding them with a sense of curiosity and openness. Reality Transurfing recognizes that our reality is not fixed, but rather a malleable construct that we can consciously shape and navigate.

Now, let's begin by guiding your body into a state of deep relaxation. Find a comfortable position, either seated or lying down, and allow your body to settle into a sense of ease and stillness. Allow your eyes to relax and slowly and comfortably close. Take a slow, deep breath in through your nose, filling your lungs with fresh, nourishing air. As you exhale through your mouth, imagine any tension, stress, or worries dissolving away, released with each outward breath. Continue this pattern of deep, mindful breathing, inhaling tranquility and exhaling any remnants of tension. Feel your body growing heavier, sinking into a state of profound peace and rest.

With your body now relaxed and your mind clear, bring your focus to the intentions you set at the beginning of this visualization. Imagine yourself embodying the qualities and attributes of your ideal level of physical fitness. Perhaps you see yourself filled with boundless energy, your body strong, resilient, and capable of taking on any challenge. Maybe you envision yourself moving with grace, ease, and fluidity, your muscles supple and responsive. Whatever your unique vision may be, allow it to take shape in your mind's eye, infusing it with vivid detail and positive emotion.

45 | PRACTICE REALITY TRANSURFING

As you hold this inspiring vision in your awareness, let's incorporate the Mirror Technique. Imagine a large, pristine mirror appearing before you. As you gaze into this mirror, see your reflection embodying the ideal physical state you just envisioned. Notice how your posture is upright and confident, your eyes sparkling with vitality, and your skin glowing with health. Observe the reflection of your body, strong and capable, a testament to your dedication and self-care. As you witness this empowered version of yourself in the mirror, understand that this is not merely a distant fantasy, but a reflection of the truth that already exists within you. Reality Transurfing teaches us that our outer world is a direct reflection of our inner state, and by shifting our thoughts, beliefs, and emotions, we can transform our reality to match our deepest desires.

Continuing to gaze at your reflection, let yourself fully absorb the energy and qualities of this optimized self. Feel the unshakable confidence, the radiant vitality, and the deep sense of self-love and acceptance that your reflection embodies. Allow these qualities to flow through the mirror and into your being, infusing every cell with their transformative power. As you merge with this reflection, affirm to yourself: "I am now aligning with my highest potential for health and fitness. My body is a miraculous vessel, capable of incredible healing, strength, and vitality. I choose to honor and nurture myself with loving thoughts, words, and actions." Feel your energy elevating as you integrate these empowering beliefs, your reflection in the mirror growing even brighter and more radiant.

As you continue to marinate in this elevated state, bring your awareness to any attachments or expectations you may be holding about the specific path or timeline for manifesting these results. The Principle of Letting Go teaches us that when we release our grip on the "how" and "when," we open ourselves up to the limitless potential of the universe to orchestrate the most perfect unfolding of our desires. Trust that by aligning yourself with the energy and essence of your goals, the most efficient and enjoyable route will be illuminated. Embrace a sense of curiosity and detachment, allowing your intentions to take root and blossom in their own organic timing.

In the philosophy of Reality Transurfing, there exists a concept known as the Alternatives Space, which is a boundless, metaphysical realm that contains every possible variation of reality, including the one in which your desired level of physical fitness is already actualized. Imagine yourself now connecting with this infinite space, feeling its vast, shimmering expanse stretched out before you. Within this space, locate the version of yourself that embodies the health, vitality and strength you aspire to. See this alternate self-radiating with an inner glow, their body perfectly conditioned and attuned. Now, begin to feel your energy merging with theirs, your frequencies synchronizing as you inherit the vibrational blueprint of this optimized physical state. Allow any sense of separation to dissolve, knowing that this reality is not some far-off possibility, but a choice you can step into at any moment.

As you absorb the energy of this elevated version of yourself, take a moment to observe any internal resistance or limiting beliefs that may arise. Perhaps there is a voice that whispers doubts about your ability to achieve your fitness goals, or a feeling of unworthiness that seeks to block your progress. Acknowledge these energies without judgment, and then consciously choose to release them, knowing they no longer serve you. Imagine these limiting patterns dissolving in the light of your expanded awareness, replaced by an unshakable conviction in your ability to shape your reality. Affirm to yourself: "I am worthy and capable of manifesting my ideal level of health and fitness. My body is a miraculous, self-healing vessel, and I honor it with loving thoughts and actions." Feel your energy recalibrating to match these empowering beliefs, any heaviness or stagnancy giving way to a renewed sense of lightness and flow.

From this place of energetic alignment, let your heart swell with gratitude for the miraculous body and life you have been gifted. Reflect on all the ways in which your physical vessel has supported you, carrying you through life's joys and challenges with unwavering resilience. Express deep appreciation for the opportunities and resources available to you in support of your fitness journey, from the nourishing food you have access to, to the inspiring teachers and role models who light your path. Acknowledge the incredible progress you have already made, and the infinite potential that lies ahead. Allow this gratitude to infuse every cell of your being, amplifying your energetic vibration and magnetizing your desired outcomes.

As you prepare to gently return your awareness to the present moment, take a few final breaths to integrate the profound shifts and insights you've experienced during this visualization. Once again, visualize the mirror before you, reflecting back to you the image of your highest potential for health and fitness. See this reflection as a living, breathing testament to your power to shape your reality through the focus of your consciousness. Affirm to yourself: "My outer world is a mirror of my inner state. As I embody the qualities of vitality, strength, and self-love, my physical reality transforms to reflect these truths back to me. I am the master architect of my life, and with each loving thought and action, I create a world of vibrant health and boundless potential." Feel these words resonating through your being, anchoring you in the unshakable knowing of your creative power.

As we come to the close of this transformative Reality Transurfing visualization, take a moment to honor yourself for the dedication and love you've shown by gifting yourself this time for self-care and growth. Trust that the intentions and visions you've planted during this practice are already taking root, and will blossom in perfect timing, in alignment with your highest good. Remember, you are the master artist of your life, and the mirror of your reality is always reflecting back to you the beauty, strength, and limitless potential that resides within.

And now, gently wiggle your fingers and toes, feeling your awareness returning fully to the physical world around you. Take a deep, cleansing breath, and when you're ready, slowly blink open your eyes, allowing them to adjust to the light. Know that the powerful energies and insights you've accessed today will continue to reverberate through every aspect of your life, guiding and supporting you on your path to physical excellence.

Thank you for honoring yourself with this sacred time of visualization and self-discovery. May your journey overflow with vibrant health, boundless energy and infinite blessings.

8. Developing the Confidence of an Articulate Public Speaker

Take a comfortable seat or lie down in a quiet space where you won't be disturbed. As we begin this visualization, set the intention to align your public speaking abilities with your desired outcomes. The practice of Reality Transurfing, which we'll be exploring today, is based on the idea that our thoughts and intentions have the power to shape our reality. By consciously directing our focus and energy, we can navigate through the infinite possibilities available to us and manifest our desired experiences. The Principle of Intention emphasizes the importance of setting clear goals and aligning our thoughts and actions with them.

Before we dive into the visualization, take a moment to relax and release any tension or distractions. Close your eyes and take a few deep breaths, allowing your body to settle into a state of calm. With each inhale, feel a sense of peace and clarity filling your being. With each exhale, let go of any stress or worries that may be weighing you down. Continue to breathe slowly and deeply, allowing your mind to become still and receptive.

Now, bring your attention to your intentions for this visualization. What do you want to achieve or experience in your public speaking journey? Perhaps it's a sense of confidence, eloquence, or the ability to captivate your audience. Take a moment to clarify your intentions, ensuring they align with your true desires. Remember, the clearer and more specific your intentions, the more powerfully they will manifest.

As you hold your intentions in mind, imagine yourself stepping into a new reality – one where you embody the qualities of a masterful public speaker. Visualize yourself standing in front of a mirror, radiating confidence and charisma. See your reflection speaking with clarity, passion, and persuasion. As you gaze into the mirror, affirm to yourself, "I am a confident and impactful speaker. My words flow effortlessly and inspire others." Feel the truth of these statements resonating within you and reflecting back through the mirror. Engage all your senses in this visualization. Feel the energy of your words, the attentiveness of your imagined audience, and the joy of sharing your message. Remember, in Reality Transurfing, the world is a mirror reflecting your inner state. By embodying the qualities you desire and aligning your thoughts and beliefs with your goals, you create a reflected reality that matches your intentions. The more vividly you imagine this reality, the more strongly you'll align with it.

As you immerse yourself in this visualization, you may notice thoughts or doubts arising, these may be fears about public speaking or limitations you've placed on yourself. Acknowledge these thoughts, but don't engage with them. Instead, gently let them go, releasing any attachment to specific outcomes or self-imposed barriers. Trust that by surrendering control and allowing your intentions to unfold naturally, you open yourself up to possibilities beyond your current perception.

In Reality Transurfing, there's also a concept known as the Alternatives Space – a realm of pure potential where all possibilities exist. Imagine yourself connecting with this space now, aligning yourself with the version of reality that best serves your public speaking intentions. Feel a sense of resonance and harmony as you tune into this optimal reality. Trust that by aligning with the Alternatives Space, you effortlessly attract the resources, opportunities, and experiences needed to manifest your goals.

As you connect with this aligned reality, take a moment to balance your energy and emotions. If any negative beliefs or limiting thoughts still linger, acknowledge them with compassion and then release them. Replace them with empowering beliefs and feelings that support your public speaking vision. Feel the truth of these supportive thoughts resonating within you and reflecting back through the mirror.

From this space of alignment and empowerment, take a moment to express gratitude for the journey you're on. Appreciate the opportunities, both past and future, to share your message and make a difference through your words. Cultivate a deep sense of appreciation for your unique voice and the impact it can have on others. As you radiate gratitude, you attract even more positive experiences and abundance into your reality.

As the visualization comes to a close, take a few deep breaths and gently bring your awareness back to the present moment. Before opening your eyes, mentally affirm that you're integrating the qualities and experiences from the visualization into your being. Know that you can return to this state of clarity and confidence whenever you need. Trust that your intentions are already manifesting, and that the universe is conspiring to support your public speaking success.

When you're ready, slowly open your eyes, carrying the energy of empowerment and inspiration with you. Remember, the reality you've envisioned is not separate from you – it's a reflection of your inner state. By aligning your thoughts, beliefs, and actions with your desired outcomes, you become the masterful speaker you've always had the potential to be. The mirror principle suggests that as you embody confidence and eloquence within, your external reality will mirror those qualities back to you.

Thank you for dedicating this time to your personal growth and evolution. Know that with each visualization and each speaking opportunity, you're strengthening your ability to manifest your dreams. Trust in the power of your intentions and enjoy the unfolding journey of becoming an extraordinary public speaker.

9. Getting Rid of Stress

Find a quiet and comfortable space where you can sit or lie down without distractions. Allow yourself to settle into a relaxed position, taking a few deep breaths to release any tension in your body and mind. Allow your eyes to softly close.

As you exhale, feel yourself letting go of any worries or concerns, knowing that this time is dedicated to your well-being and inner peace. Set the intention to align yourself with a reality where stress dissolves and tranquility prevails. Reality Transurfing reminds us that our thoughts and beliefs shape our experiences, and by consciously focusing on our desired outcomes, we can navigate the infinite field of possibilities and manifest the reality we desire.

Continue to breathe slowly and deeply, allowing each exhale to carry away any remnants of stress or negativity. Feel your body sinking into a state of deep relaxation, as if you are being gently cradled by a warm, comforting energy. With each breath, your mind becomes quieter and more still, releasing any racing thoughts or mental chatter. Embrace the peace that arises in the space between your thoughts.

Now, bring your attention to your intentions for this visualization. Consider the areas of your life where you wish to experience greater ease, harmony, and inner peace. Visualize yourself embodying the qualities of calmness, resilience, and unwavering strength. See yourself moving through challenges with grace and composure, maintaining a centered and balanced state of being. The more clearly and vividly you can imagine yourself living in alignment with your intentions, the more powerfully you will attract and manifest that reality.

Imagine yourself standing in front of a large, pristine mirror. As you gaze into the mirror, you see a reflection of yourself that exudes an aura of serenity and inner peace. This is your

THE MIRROR TECHNIQUE | 54

true self, the version of you that remains unaffected by external stressors and challenges. Take a moment to connect with this reflection, affirming silently, "I am the master of my inner world. I choose peace in every moment." As you hold this connection, visualize a stressful situation appearing in the mirror. Observe how your mirror self navigates the situation with remarkable ease and composure. Notice the steady, even breath, the clear and focused mind, and the emanation of an unwavering calm. As your mirror self embodies these qualities, witness how the outer reflection begins to shift and transform, aligning with your inner state of tranquility. The stressful situation dissolves, replaced by a reality were peace and harmony reign supreme. The mirror now reflects back to you a world where challenges are met with grace, and stress dissipates in the presence of your inner strength. Remember that the Principle of Mirroring works because our outer world is a direct reflection of our inner state, by cultivating peace within, we have the power to transform our external reality.

As you hold this vision of your peaceful reflection, release any attachment to specific outcomes or timelines. Trust that the universe is conspiring in your favor, orchestrating the perfect unfolding of events to support your highest good. Surrender the need to control or force outcomes, knowing that by letting go, you create space for the natural flow of abundance and positive experiences.

Now, connect with the Alternatives Space, the realm of infinite possibilities where all potentials exist. Imagine a version of yourself that is already living in complete alignment with your intentions—calm, centered, and thriving in the face of any challenge. Feel the energy of this alternative self merging with your current reality, infusing you with the qualities and experiences you desire. Allow yourself to fully embody this version of yourself, knowing that it is not a distant possibility, but a reality that you can step into right now.

Take a moment to assess your inner state, noticing any thoughts or emotions that arise. If you detect any negative or limiting beliefs, gently acknowledge them and then release them with your exhale. Replace these thoughts with empowering affirmations and beliefs that support your desired reality. Repeat silently to yourself, "I am capable of handling any challenge with ease and grace. I choose to radiate peace and calm in every moment." Feel the vibrational shift within you as you align your energy with these empowering statements.

As you continue to embody this state of peace and alignment, allow a sense of deep gratitude to fill your heart. Give thanks for the present moment and all the blessings in your life, both big and small. Recognize that even challenges and obstacles serve a purpose in your growth and evolution. Cultivate an attitude of appreciation for the journey you are on, knowing that each step is leading you towards your highest potential.

As you prepare to gently return your awareness to the present moment, take a few final deep breaths, integrating the experiences and insights you've gained during this visualization. Allow the feelings of peace, resilience, and inner strength to permeate every cell of your being, knowing that they are now a part of who you are. Recognize that you have the power to access this state of calm and clarity whenever you need it, simply by returning to your breath and remembering the truth of who you are.

When you feel ready, slowly begin to bring your awareness back to your physical body and surroundings. Wiggle your fingers and toes, feeling a renewed sense of energy and vitality flowing through you. Take a final deep breath, and gently open your eyes, carrying with you the unshakable knowing that you are the creator of your reality. Remember that stress reduction is an ongoing practice, and by consistently choosing thoughts, emotions, and actions that align with your desired outcomes, you will cultivate a life of lasting peace and well-being.

Thank yourself for making the time to go within and connect with your inner wisdom. Trust in the journey of your life, knowing that the universe is always supporting and guiding you towards your highest good. Carry this sense of peace and alignment with you as you move forward, radiating your light and positivity into the world around you.

10. Overcoming Fears

Welcome to this transformative visualization experience, where we will harness the power of Reality Transurfing to overcome our fears and manifest the life we truly desire. Let us begin by setting a clear intention: to face our fears with unwavering courage and emerge victorious, empowered, and transformed. Reality Transurfing recognizes the fundamental principle that our thoughts, beliefs, and intentions shape our reality. By aligning ourselves with the reality we wish to experience, we can create profound and lasting changes in our lives.

To begin this journey, find a comfortable position and allow your body to settle into a state of deep relaxation. Slowly close your eyes. Take a slow, deep breath in through your nose, filling your lungs with rejuvenating air. As you exhale through your mouth, feel any tension, stress, or worries melting away, released with each outward breath. Continue this gentle rhythm of breathing, allowing each inhale to draw in tranquility and each exhale to release any remaining tightness in your body. Feel your muscles softening, your mind quieting, and your entire being surrendering to a state of profound peace and relaxation.

As you rest in this space of deep relaxation, bring your awareness to your intentions for this visualization. What fears do you wish to overcome? What limiting beliefs do you want to release? What qualities and experiences do you desire to manifest in your life? Take a moment to connect with your inner wisdom and clarify your intentions. Visualize yourself embodying the attributes of courage, resilience, and triumph. See yourself navigating challenges with grace, ease, and unwavering determination. Feel the power of your intentions radiating from within, permeating every cell of your being.

Now, let your imagination guide you to a serene and enchanting space, a realm of infinite possibilities. As you explore this inner landscape, you come across a magnificent, ornate mirror standing before you. This is no ordinary mirror; it is a powerful reflection of your inner world and the reality you are creating. Approach the mirror with a sense of curiosity and reverence, and take a moment to observe your reflection. Notice how the mirror reflects not only your physical appearance but also your thoughts, emotions, beliefs, and aspirations. The Principle of the Mirror suggests that our outer world is a direct reflection of our inner state, and by transforming our inner reality, we can create profound changes in our external experience.

As you gaze into the mirror, connect with your reflection and affirm to yourself, "I am the master of my reality. I choose courage over fear." Witness your reflection begin to transform, embodying the qualities of fearlessness, strength, and unshakable confidence. See yourself standing tall, radiating an aura of self-assurance and determination. Your eyes sparkle with the knowledge that you have the power to overcome any obstacle and manifest your deepest desires. The mirror reflects back to you the image of your triumphant self, having conquered your fears and stepped into your greatness.

As you witness your empowered reflection in the mirror, allow yourself to release any attachment to specific outcomes or limiting beliefs that may have held you back in the past. Embrace the understanding that the universe is conspiring in your favor, and trust in the natural flow of reality. Surrender any need for control or rigidity, and open yourself to the limitless possibilities that await you. As you let go and relinquish your grip on how things should unfold, you create space for miracles and serendipitous opportunities to enter your life.

With a deep breath, imagine yourself stepping through the mirror and into the Alternatives Space, this is the realm where all versions of reality exist simultaneously. In this space, you have the power to align yourself with the version of reality where your fears have been overcome and your desired experiences are already manifest. Feel the emotions of triumph, courage, and unshakable self-belief flowing through every fiber of your being. Allow these empowering energies to permeate your consciousness, anchoring them deep within your soul.

As you bask in the energy of your desired reality, take a moment to consciously release any lingering negative or limiting beliefs that may have been blocking your path. Visualize these beliefs as heavy weights or dark clouds, and with each exhalation, watch them dissipate and dissolve, replaced by an influx of empowering thoughts and emotions. Affirm to yourself, "I release all that no longer serves me, and I embrace the limitless potential within me." Feel a renewed sense of lightness, clarity, and inner peace as you align your energy with your highest aspirations.

In this space of alignment and empowerment, take a moment to cultivate a deep sense of gratitude for the abundance, opportunities, and blessings already present in your life. Acknowledge the incredible journey you have undertaken and appreciate the growth, wisdom, and strength you have gained along the way. Feel a profound sense of appreciation for the challenges you have overcome, knowing that they have shaped you into the resilient and courageous being you are today. The Principle of Gratitude emphasizes the transformative power of appreciating and acknowledging the good in our lives, as it amplifies our positive energy and attracts even more abundance and blessings into our experience.

As you prepare to conclude this profound visualization, take a few moments to integrate the insights, energies, and transformations you have experienced. Allow the feelings of empowerment, courage, and alignment to permeate every cell of your being, anchoring them deep within your consciousness. Affirm to yourself, "I am courageous, I am strong, and I am aligned with my highest reality." Know that you have the power to carry these qualities with you as you navigate your daily life, radiating your inner light and manifesting your desires with ease and grace.

As you gently begin to bring your awareness back to the present moment, take a deep breath and slowly open your eyes. Carry the feelings of triumph, self-belief, and alignment with you as you re-engage with the world around you. Remember that your outer reality is a direct reflection of your inner state, and by nurturing the seeds of courage and confidence within, you will witness your external world blossoming in miraculous ways. Trust in the journey, knowing that the universe is supporting you every step of the way, and that your fears are merely stepping stones to your greatest triumphs.

Thank you for dedicating this time to your personal growth and transformation. May you continue to embrace your innate power, wisdom, and resilience as you navigate the path ahead. Remember that you are the master of your reality, and with each courageous step, you are manifesting a life of boundless joy, abundance, and fulfillment. Carry this knowing with you, and let your light shine brightly for all to see.

11. Cultivating Mindfulness

Welcome to this transformative visualization session, where we will delve into the profound principles of Reality Transurfing to cultivate a deep sense of mindfulness and align ourselves with our most cherished desires. Reality Transurfing is a powerful framework that illuminates the fundamental truth that our thoughts and intentions possess the remarkable ability to shape and mold our experiences. By focusing our attention on the end goal, we invite the universe to gracefully arrange the path that leads us there. As we embark on this journey together, set a clear intention to be fully present, open, and receptive to the insights and experiences that will unfold during this sacred time. Allow yourself to let go of any preconceived notions or expectations, and simply surrender to the wisdom and guidance that will naturally arise.

To begin, find a comfortable position that allows your body to relax completely, whether seated or lying down. Close your eyes and take a few slow, deep breaths, inhaling the energy of peace and exhaling any lingering tension or stress. With each breath, feel your body surrendering to the support beneath you, sinking deeper into a state of profound relaxation and receptivity. Notice any areas of your body that may be holding onto tension, and consciously release them with each exhalation. As you continue to breathe deeply, feel a sense of calm and tranquility washing over you, preparing you for the transformative experience ahead.

As you settle into this relaxed state, bring your awareness to your intentions for this visualization. What is it that you truly wish to cultivate or experience in your life? Is it a greater sense of clarity, a deeper connection to presence, or an unshakable inner peace? Take a moment to visualize these intentions as already manifested, fully embodied within you. Feel the vibrant emotions and sensations associated with living in complete alignment with your deepest desires. Imagine how it would feel to wake up each day with a profound sense of purpose, knowing that you are living in harmony with your highest truth. Allow these positive emotions to permeate every cell of your being, anchoring them deeply within your consciousness.

Now, imagine yourself standing before a magnificent, ornate mirror. As you gaze into its reflective surface, you behold a stunning reflection of yourself, radiating the essence of your desired reality. Take in the details of your reflection, noticing how it embodies the qualities and experiences you wish to manifest. Observe the unwavering confidence, the radiant joy, and the grounded presence that emanates from your reflection. As you continue to focus on this image, remember that your outer world is a direct reflection of your inner state. Just as the mirror reflects your image with perfect clarity, your reality reflects your thoughts, beliefs, and attitudes with unwavering precision. Embrace the power of this realization, knowing that by shifting your inner world, you have the ability to transform your external experiences in profound ways.

As you immerse yourself in the visualization of your desired reality in the mirror, release any attachment to specific outcomes or perceived limitations. Surrender control, trusting in the natural flow and wisdom of the universe, knowing that it is always conspiring in your favor. Let go of any resistance or doubts that may arise, allowing yourself to fully embrace the infinite possibilities available to you. Trust that the universe has a plan for you that is far greater than anything you could imagine, and that by aligning yourself with this higher intelligence, you open the doorway to miraculous experiences and synchronicities.

Connect now with the Alternatives Space, a realm of pure potential and infinite possibilities. This is a dimension where all realities exist simultaneously, and where you can align yourself with the versions of reality that best serve your intentions and your highest self. Feel the vibrant energy of this space flowing through you, supporting and guiding you towards your desired outcomes. Imagine a vast, luminous field stretching out before you, filled with countless shimmering threads representing different potential realities. With a sense of curiosity and openness, allow yourself to be drawn towards the threads that resonate most strongly with your deepest desires and aspirations.

Take a moment to balance your energy and emotions, releasing any negative or limiting beliefs that may be blocking your desired reality. Cultivate a deep sense of inner peace and harmony, knowing that you have the power to choose your thoughts and responses in any situation. Visualize a brilliant, golden light emanating from your heart center, expanding to fill your entire being and radiating out into the world around you. As this light grows stronger and brighter, feel any lingering negativity or self-doubt dissolving in its presence, replaced by an unshakable sense of love, compassion, and acceptance for yourself and others.

As you prepare to conclude this visualization, take a moment to express gratitude for the abundance and opportunities already present in your life. Cultivate an attitude of deep appreciation for the journey you are on, trusting that every experience, whether perceived as positive or negative, is ultimately contributing to your growth and evolution. Reflect on the many blessings and miracles that have already unfolded in your life, and open your heart to receive even more. Offer a silent prayer of thanks to the universe for its unwavering support and guidance, knowing that you are forever held in its loving embrace.

Gently begin to integrate the insights and experiences gained during this visualization into your daily life. Carry the feelings of empowerment, presence, and alignment with you as you navigate your day-to-day experiences. Remember that your outer world is a direct reflection of your inner state, and by cultivating mindfulness and positive intentions, you have the power to create profound shifts in your reality.

As you slowly return your awareness to the present moment, take a deep breath and gently open your eyes. Carry the peace and presence cultivated during this visualization with you throughout your day, allowing it to infuse your interactions and experiences with a greater sense of clarity and purpose. Trust in the journey and know that you are exactly where you need to be, even if it may not always feel that way. Remember that every challenge and obstacle you face is an opportunity for growth and self-discovery, and that by approaching life with a sense of curiosity and openness, you will always find the wisdom and guidance you need.

Remember, the power to shape your reality lies within you. By aligning your thoughts, beliefs, and actions with your deepest intentions and desires, you become the master of your own reality. Continue to practice these principles of Reality Transurfing, and trust that the universe will conspire to support you every step of the way. Embrace the journey with open arms, knowing that each moment is an opportunity to create the life of your dreams. Thank you for your presence and commitment to your personal growth and transformation. May you continue to walk the path of mindfulness and alignment, and may your life be filled with an abundance of joy, love, and fulfillment.

12. Creating Your Dream Career

Welcome to this powerful visualization designed to support you in navigating your career transition with ease, confidence, and alignment. In this practice, we will harness the principles of Reality Transurfing, a transformative approach to manifesting your desired reality. By engaging in this visualization, you will learn to clarify your career aspirations, align your energy with your desired outcomes, and trust in the universe's support as you embark on this exciting new chapter. So, find a comfortable position, close your eyes, and let's begin this journey of self-discovery and manifestation.

Find a quiet and comfortable space where you can sit or lie down without interruptions. Close your eyes and take a few deep, slow breaths, allowing your body to relax with each exhale. As you continue to breathe, set the intention to navigate your career transition with ease, confidence, and trust in the universe's support. Remind yourself that your thoughts and intentions have the power to shape your reality, and by focusing on your desired outcomes, you align yourself with the path of least resistance.

Now, bring your awareness to your physical body, starting from the tips of your toes and gradually moving up to the crown of your head. As you focus on each part of your body, consciously release any tension or tightness you may be holding. Feel your feet and legs grow heavy and relaxed, your hips and lower back softening into the surface beneath you. Notice your belly and chest rise and fall with each breath, allowing any tension in your shoulders, neck, and jaw to melt away. As your body slips into a state of deep relaxation, feel your mind becoming calm, clear, and receptive to the transformative power of this visualization.

With your mind and body in a state of relaxation, take a moment to clarify your intentions for your career transition.

Imagine your ideal job or career path in vivid detail, focusing on the feelings of fulfillment, joy, growth, and abundance that come with it. Visualize yourself thriving in this new role, confidently navigating challenges, and seizing opportunities for success. The more specific and emotionally charged your intentions, the more powerful their impact on your reality. Feel the excitement, passion, and sense of purpose that comes with aligning your career with your deepest values and aspirations.

Now, begin to visualize yourself in your desired career reality. Imagine a large, ornate mirror appearing before you, its surface shimmering with potential. The frame is intricately carved, adorned with symbols of growth, prosperity, and achievement. As you step closer, you feel a magnetic pull drawing you toward the reflective glass.

Gaze deeply into the mirror and witness your reflection transforming into the image of your professional self—poised, confident, and radiating success. Your posture is upright, your shoulders back, and your head held high. Your eyes sparkle with determination and purpose. You exude an aura of self-assurance and capability.

Now, see yourself stepping through the mirror and onto a path that leads to your new career. Each step you take is filled with purpose and determination, propelling you forward with unwavering faith. As you walk, visualize doors of opportunity opening before you, revealing new connections, projects, and possibilities that align with your goals. Feel the warmth of the sun on your face and the gentle breeze at your back, symbolizing the universe's support and guidance on your journey.

As you continue along the path, focus on the feeling of being welcomed and celebrated in your new role. Imagine your colleagues and superiors greeting you with genuine smiles, appreciation, and recognition of your unique talents and contributions. Feel the sense of belonging and camaraderie that comes with being part of a team that values and supports your growth. Allow your inner state to align with the natural flow of career progression, trusting that your transition is unfolding in perfect timing and alignment with your highest good.

With each step, repeat the affirmation, "My world responds to my intention. I transition to my new career with grace, ease, and abundance." Feel the power of these words resonating through your being, aligning your energy and vibration with the reality of your desires. As you repeat the affirmation, notice your reflection in the mirror becoming clearer, more vibrant, and more aligned with your ideal career self. The image in the mirror serves as a powerful reminder that your outer world is a reflection of your inner state, and by cultivating a positive, confident, and abundant mindset, you naturally attract experiences that match your intentions.

As you near the end of the path, create a vivid mental slide, this can be a snapshot of yourself thriving in your new career. See yourself engaged in meaningful work, collaborating with inspiring colleagues, and making a positive impact in your field. Notice the details of your surroundings, the expressions on people's faces, and the sense of fulfillment and joy that permeates the scene. Step into this slide, fully immersing yourself in the experience, and allow the feelings of success, gratitude, and abundance to wash over you. Engage all your senses, making the visualization as real and tangible as possible. The more vivid and emotionally charged your visualization, the more powerfully it impacts your reality.

As you bask in the glow of your desired career reality, let go of any attachment to specific outcomes or timelines. Trust that the universe has a perfect plan for your transition and that everything is unfolding in divine order. Release any fears, doubts, or limiting beliefs that may arise, knowing that they are simply temporary obstacles on your path to success. Embrace the uncertainty and challenges as opportunities for growth and learning, trusting in your resilience and ability to adapt. Surrender control and allow yourself to flow with the current of your life, knowing that you are being guided towards your highest good and the fulfillment of your career dreams.

Now, imagine yourself expanding your awareness beyond the visualization and connecting with the vast expanse of the Alternatives Space. In this realm of infinite possibilities, your desired career reality already exists, pulsing with life and potential. Feel the boundless energy of the Alternatives Space flowing through you, filling you with the confidence, creativity, and inspiration to manifest your goals. Imagine yourself merging with the version of you that is already living your ideal career, absorbing the qualities, skills, and experiences that define your success. Allow yourself to embody the energy and vibration of your future self, anchoring it in your present moment awareness. By aligning with the version of reality that already holds your desired outcome, you can accelerate your manifestation process and bring your dreams into physical reality more efficiently.

As you align with your desired career reality, take a moment to assess your energy and emotional state. Notice any negative or limiting beliefs that may be lurking in the shadows of your mind, and consciously choose to release them. Replace these limiting thoughts with empowering affirmations and beliefs that support your growth and success. Cultivate a deep sense of gratitude for the experiences, lessons, and opportunities that have brought you to this pivotal moment in your career journey. Acknowledge the challenges you've overcome and the strengths you've developed, knowing that every step has been an essential part of your unique path. By managing your energy and maintaining a positive, grateful mindset, you create a powerful vibrational match for the reality you desire to manifest.

As you prepare to conclude your visualization, take a final moment to express gratitude for the abundance, support, and opportunities that are already flowing into your life. Give thanks for the people, resources, and synchronicities that are conspiring to support your career transition and guide you towards your highest potential. Cultivate a deep appreciation for the journey itself, recognizing that every step, whether challenging or joyful, is an essential part of your growth and evolution. Embrace the present moment, knowing that your desired career reality is already unfolding, and trust in the perfection of your unique path. As you focus on appreciation and abundance, you attract more of the same into your reality and this creates a positive feedback loop of manifestation.

Take a deep breath and allow the insights, energy, and inspiration from your visualization to integrate fully into your being. Know that the powerful intentions you've set and the vivid visualizations you've created have already begun to shape your reality, aligning you with the people, opportunities, and circumstances that will support your career transition. Carry the feelings of empowerment, trust, and abundance with you as you navigate this exciting new chapter, remembering that you are the creator of your reality and have the power to manifest your deepest career aspirations.

Gently wiggle your fingers and toes, taking a few deep breaths as you slowly return your awareness to the present moment. When you feel ready, open your eyes, feeling refreshed, energized, and inspired to take aligned action towards your career goals. Trust in the power of your intentions, the guidance of the universe, and the strength of your own spirit as you navigate this transitional phase with grace, ease, and unwavering faith. Remember, your reality is a mirror of your inner world, and by cultivating a positive, abundant, and purposeful mindset, you naturally attract experiences and opportunities that reflect your deepest desires and aspirations.

As you move through your day, carry the energy and insights from this visualization with you, allowing them to infuse your thoughts, words, and actions with the vibration of success, fulfillment, and abundance. Stay open to the signs, synchronicities, and opportunities that the universe presents, knowing that they are guiding you towards your highest path and the full expression of your career potential. Trust in the journey, embrace the challenges as opportunities for growth, and celebrate the victories, both big and small, along the way.

Remember, your career transition is a sacred journey of self-discovery, growth, and alignment with your true purpose. By staying connected to your intentions, nurturing a positive and grateful mindset, and taking inspired action, you are co-creating a reality that reflects your deepest desires and aspirations. Trust in the power of your own transformation and the unwavering support of the universe as you step into this new chapter with confidence, courage, and an open heart. Your ideal career reality is already unfolding, and with each step, you are aligning yourself with the path of greatness, purpose, and fulfillment that is your birthright.

13. Manifesting Spiritual Growth

Welcome to this guided visualization for spiritual growth, inspired by the principles of Reality Transurfing. Reality Transurfing is a philosophy that suggests our reality is shaped by our thoughts, beliefs, and intentions. If we consciously align our inner state with our desired outcomes, we will navigate the infinite possibilities of existence and manifest our ideal reality. The Principle of Intention is at the heart of this practice.

To begin, find a quiet, comfortable space where you can relax without interruptions. You may choose to sit or lie down, whichever allows you to be most at ease. Close your eyes and take a few deep, cleansing breaths. As you inhale, feel your body filling with peaceful, calming energy. As you exhale, release any tension, stress, or distractions that may be present. With each breath, allow yourself to sink deeper into a state of relaxation and receptivity, feeling your body grow heavy and your mind become quiet.

In this peaceful state, take a moment to connect with your intentions for this visualization. Consider the aspects of your spiritual growth that you wish to focus on. Perhaps you seek to deepen your connection with the Divine, cultivate greater compassion and understanding, or experience profound insights and revelations. Whatever your intentions may be, hold them gently in your heart, knowing that clarity and alignment between your desires and your higher self are key to manifesting your ideal reality.

Now, allow your imagination to take you on a journey to a sacred, ethereal space that embodies your ideal environment for spiritual growth. This space is unique to you, and may take any form that resonates with your soul. Perhaps you find yourself in a serene, lush garden, filled with fragrant flowers, bubbling fountains, and gentle birdsong. Or maybe you are transported to a majestic mountain top, surrounded by

THE MIRROR TECHNIQUE | 72

towering peaks, crisp air, and a vast, open sky. Wherever your inner wisdom guides you, trust that this space is perfectly suited for your spiritual journey.

As you explore this sacred space, engage all of your senses to fully immerse yourself in the experience. See the vivid colors and intricate details of your surroundings, noticing how the light seems to shimmer and dance across the landscape. Hear the soothing sounds of nature, perhaps the whisper of the wind through the trees or the gentle babbling of a nearby stream. Feel the soft, nurturing ground beneath your feet, and the warm, comforting air enveloping your skin. Allow yourself to be fully present in this moment, savoring the peace and tranquility that surrounds you.

As you continue to journey through this space, you notice a large, ornate mirror standing before you. This mirror is no ordinary reflection; it is a powerful symbol of your inner world, capable of reflecting your deepest thoughts, beliefs, and attitudes. Approach the mirror with reverence and curiosity, knowing that it holds the key to unlocking your spiritual potential.

Gaze deeply into the mirror's surface, and see yourself reflected back in its shimmering depths. But this is not your ordinary, everyday self. Instead, you see the embodiment of your highest spiritual potential, radiant and illuminated from within. Notice the wisdom and compassion that shine from your eyes, the gentle smile that graces your lips, and the aura of peace and love that surrounds you. This is the truth of who you are, beyond any limitations, fears, or doubts.

As you continue to gaze into the mirror, allow your desired spiritual qualities and experiences to be reflected back to you. See yourself embodying profound peace, unconditional love, and a deep, unshakable connection to the Divine. Watch as the mirror reveals the reality of your spiritual growth and transformation, showing you the boundless potential that lies within you. Remember, the world around you is a mirror, constantly reflecting your inner state. By focusing your intentions and beliefs on your desired qualities and experiences, you are actively shaping your reality.

While immersed in this powerful reflection, you may notice thoughts, attachments, or limitations arising in your mind. Acknowledge these with gentleness and compassion, understanding that they are simply old patterns that no longer serve you. As they arise, release them with each exhalation, allowing them to dissipate like mist in the morning sun. Trust in the natural flow of reality and surrender control to a higher wisdom, knowing that by letting go of resistance and embracing acceptance, you open yourself to limitless possibilities.

In this state of openness and surrender, feel yourself connecting with the Alternative Space, a realm of pure potential and infinite possibilities. This space exists beyond the confines of time and space, and is accessible to you whenever you align your consciousness with its vibration. As you connect with the Alternatives Space, feel yourself resonating with the versions of reality that best serve your spiritual growth and highest good. Trust that the universe is conspiring in your favor, and that everything you need for your journey is available to you, waiting to be claimed.

As you prepare to integrate your experiences from this visualization, take a moment to check in with your energy and emotional state. If you notice any lingering negativity or limiting beliefs, gently acknowledge them and consciously choose to replace them with empowering, affirming thoughts. Focus on cultivating a state of balance, harmony, and inner peace, knowing that by managing your energy and vibration, you attune yourself to the realities that resonate with your desired outcomes.

Before returning to your everyday reality, take a moment to express gratitude for the abundance and opportunities present in your life. Cultivate an attitude of deep appreciation for the journey you are on, recognizing that every experience, whether challenging or joyful, is an opportunity for growth and learning. Gratitude is a powerful force that attracts more positivity and blessings into your reality, so allow yourself to marinate in this feeling of appreciation, letting it fill every cell of your being.

As you gently begin to integrate the insights and experiences from this visualization into your conscious awareness, allow the feelings of empowerment, clarity, and alignment to permeate your being. Know that you have the power to shape your reality through your intentions, beliefs, and actions, and that by carrying this wisdom with you into your daily life, you are stepping into your role as the creator of your own journey.

When you feel ready, take a deep, cleansing breath and slowly open your eyes, allowing your awareness to return to the present moment. Feel grounded, centered, and filled with a renewed sense of purpose and possibility, knowing that the insights and experiences from this visualization will continue to guide and inspire you on your path.

Remember that your spiritual growth is a lifelong journey, and that each step, no matter how small, is a step towards your highest potential. Trust in the journey, trust in yourself, and trust in the wisdom of the universe, knowing that you are exactly where you need to be, and that everything is unfolding in perfect divine order.

Thank you for dedicating this time to your spiritual practice and personal growth. May the insights and experiences from this visualization continue

75 | PRACTICE REALITY TRANSURFING

to illuminate your path, guiding you ever closer to your true, divine self. Embrace the journey with open arms, and know that the universe is always supporting you, cheering you on, and conspiring in your favor.

14. Creating Joyful Living

Welcome to this powerful visualization on Joyful Living, inspired by the transformative principles of Reality Transurfing. This is a revolutionary approach to navigating your reality and manifesting your deepest desires by aligning your intentions with the natural flow and rhythm of the universe.

To begin this profound journey, find a quiet, comfortable space where you can sit or lie down without any interruptions or distractions. Gently close your eyes. Allow your body to settle into a deeply relaxed position, letting go of any tension, tightness, or discomfort that may be present.

Take a deep, cleansing breath, inhaling slowly and deliberately through your nose, feeling the air fill your lungs and expand your chest. As you exhale gradually through your mouth, feel your body and mind releasing any lingering stress, worries, or concerns, sinking into a state of peaceful receptivity and openness. With each subsequent breath, allow yourself to relax even more deeply, letting go of any resistance or barriers, and opening yourself up to the limitless possibilities that surround you, waiting to be explored and embraced.

As you continue to breathe slowly and deeply, bring your attention to your intention for this visualization. What is it that you truly desire to experience, manifest, or cultivate in your life? It could be a profound sense of joy and happiness, an abundance of love, warmth, and connection, or a feeling of deep fulfillment, purpose, and meaning. Whatever your intention may be, allow it to crystallize clearly and vividly in your mind, feeling its essence resonate within every cell, fiber, and atom of your being.

Now, let your imagination guide you on a captivating inner journey of self-discovery and transformation. Visualize yourself standing in front of an ornate, full-length mirror, its frame adorned with intricate designs and symbols that speak to your soul. As you gaze into the mirror, you see a reflection of yourself that radiates pure joy, peace, and contentment. This is a version of yourself that embodies all the qualities, attributes, and experiences you wish to manifest in your reality. Notice the way your reflection stands tall and proud, shoulders back and head held high, exuding an aura of unshakable confidence, positivity, and self-assurance. See the warm, genuine smile on your face, reflecting the deep sense of happiness, fulfillment, and inner peace that resides within the very core of your being.

As you continue to observe your reflection, remember that your outer world is a direct mirror and reflection of your inner state. This is because the thoughts, beliefs, and emotions you nurture and cultivate within yourself are reflected back to you in the reality you experience, shaping your life in profound and meaningful ways.

While you explore this rich inner landscape of potential and possibility, you may notice thoughts, doubts, or limitations arising, like fleeting shadows or whispers in the background. These may manifest as subtle changes or distortions in your reflection, such as a slight furrowing of the brow, a dimming of your radiant smile, or a momentary flicker of uncertainty in your eyes. Acknowledge these thoughts and feelings without judgment or resistance, understanding that they are simply a natural part of the human experience, a testament to your growth and evolution. As you breathe deeply and mindfully, imagine exhaling these limiting beliefs, fears, and doubts, watching them dissipate like wisps of smoke or mist in the mirror, fading into the ether. Trust that the universe has a perfect plan and purpose for you, and surrender any need to control or dictate the outcome, knowing that all is unfolding in divine timing and alignment.

Now, imagine yourself connecting with the boundless potential and infinite possibilities of the Alternatives Space.

This is a realm where all potentialities exist simultaneously, and where you have the innate power and ability to choose the reality that aligns with your deepest desires, aspirations, and intentions. As you gaze into the mirror, see your reflection shifting, morphing, and transforming, embodying the qualities, experiences, and attributes you wish to manifest and call forth into your life. Notice how your reflection becomes even more vibrant, radiant, and alive, emanating an aura of pure joy, abundance, fulfillment, and alignment. Feel yourself resonating and harmonizing with this version of reality, knowing that it is already a part of you, waiting to be expressed, celebrated, and made manifest in your physical world. The concept of the Alternatives Space, which is a core philosophy in Reality Transurfing, reminds us that we are not limited or constrained by our current circumstances or conditions. Rather, we have the power to consciously shape, mold, and create our reality through our choices, intentions, and unwavering belief in the goodness and abundance of life.

As you align yourself with your desired reality, take a moment to balance and harmonize your energy and emotions, bringing them into a state of perfect equilibrium and flow. Release any lingering negative or limiting beliefs, watching them fade away and dissolve in the mirror, like mist under the warmth and radiance of the rising sun. Replace them with empowering, uplifting thoughts and feelings of abundance, gratitude, and unwavering trust in the benevolence of the universe. See these positive qualities and attributes reflected back to you, amplifying their presence and influence in your life, permeating every aspect of your being.

Now, take a moment to express heartfelt, sincere gratitude for all the blessings, opportunities, and experiences that are already present and abundant in your life. Acknowledge the unique, one-of-a-kind journey you are on, appreciating and honoring the growth, lessons, and moments of joy, love, and connection along the way. Cultivate a profound sense of appreciation, wonder, and awe for the abundance and beauty that surrounds you, knowing that there is always more on the horizon, waiting to be discovered, embraced, and celebrated. As you express gratitude and appreciation, notice how your reflection in the mirror becomes even more radiant, joyful, and luminous, reflecting the abundance, positivity, and grace you are emanating from the very essence of your being.

As you prepare to return to your waking reality, take a moment to fully integrate, embody, and anchor the insights, realizations, and experiences from this powerful, transformative visualization. Feel the empowerment, confidence, and unwavering alignment with your desired reality, knowing that it is already unfolding in perfect divine timing, orchestrated by the loving intelligence of the universe. Carry these feelings of joy, positivity, gratitude, and faith with you as you navigate the beautiful tapestry of your daily life, trusting that the universe is constantly conspiring in your favor, working tirelessly behind the scenes to bring your dreams, desires, and aspirations to fruition. Remember that your outer world is a mirror and reflection of your inner state, and by cultivating joyful, expansive, and loving energy within yourself, you will witness these qualities and attributes reflected back to you in the reality you experience, like a beautiful dance of co-creation and manifestation.

When you feel ready and grounded, gently bring your awareness back to the present moment, taking a deep, cleansing breath and slowly opening your eyes, allowing the world to come into focus once more. As you return to your waking reality, hold fast to the knowing that you are the master and creator of your own reality, wielding the power to shape your experiences, circumstances, and conditions through your intentions, choices, and energy. Trust in the perfect unfolding of your journey, knowing that you are always supported, guided, and loved by the infinite wisdom and intelligence of the universe, which seeks only your highest good, greatest joy, and most authentic expression.

Thank you for dedicating this sacred time and space to your personal growth. May you continue to navigate your reality with grace, ease, joy, and alignment, witnessing your desired qualities, experiences, and attributes reflected back to you in the mirror of your life, like a beautiful testament to the power of your thoughts, beliefs, and emotions. Embrace your innate power and gifts as a conscious creator and master manifestor, knowing that you are infinitely capable of bringing forth a reality that fills your heart with joy, purpose, meaning, and abundance, now and always. Trust in the journey, trust in yourself, and trust in the unwavering love and support of the universe, as you continue to grow, evolve, and manifest a life beyond your wildest dreams and imaginings.

15. Manifesting Perfect Health

Welcome to this powerful Reality Transurfing visualization for embodying perfect health. As we prepare to embark on this transformative journey, let's take a moment to understand the core principles of Reality Transurfing. This remarkable approach teaches us that our thoughts and intentions have the incredible ability to shape our reality. By aligning our inner state with our desired outcomes, we gain the power to navigate the infinite possibilities available to us and manifest the life we truly desire. The

To begin, find a comfortable position, either seated or lying down, and allow your body to relax completely. Gently close your eyes. Take a few deep, slow breaths, focusing on the sensation of the air moving in and out of your lungs. With each exhale, release any tension or stress you may be holding onto, letting it dissolve into the earth beneath you. Feel your muscles softening, your mind becoming calm and centered, and your entire being surrendering to the sacred present moment.

Now, set a clear and specific intention for this visualization. Ask yourself, what does perfect health truly mean to you? Take a moment to connect deeply with your vision of optimal well-being. Visualize yourself living a life filled with vitality, energy, and radiance. See yourself engaging in activities that nourish your body, mind, and soul, such as eating wholesome foods, exercising with joy and enthusiasm, and getting restorative sleep. Feel the pure joy, profound gratitude, and deep sense of fulfillment that comes with experiencing optimal health in every aspect of your being.

Imagine yourself standing in front of a large, ornate mirror, its surface shimmering with an ethereal, mystical glow. As you gaze into the mirror, you see a reflection of yourself radiating perfect health. Your skin is glowing with vitality, your eyes are sparkling with vibrant energy, and your body is strong, flexible, and vibrant. Notice how your posture is upright and confident, reflecting your inner state of well-being and self-assurance. As you continue to observe your reflection, see the mirror expand and transform, revealing a world that reflects your deepest thoughts and attitudes about health. The Principle of the Mirror states that our external reality is a direct reflection of our inner world, and by focusing intently on the reality we wish to create, we can manifest it powerfully in our lives.

In this mirror world, you find yourself surrounded by an environment that supports and nurtures your well-being in every way imaginable. The air is crisp, clean, and invigorating, filling your lungs with life-giving oxygen. The water is pure, crystal-clear, and deeply hydrating, nourishing your body on a cellular level. The food is vibrant, colorful, and bursting with nutrients, providing you with the essential building blocks for optimal health. You see yourself engaging in activities that bring you immense joy and vitality, such as walking in nature, running, or spending quality time with loved ones. Notice how the people in this mirror world reflect your own positive attitudes and beliefs about health, supporting and encouraging you on your journey with their own radiant well-being.

As you immerse yourself fully in this reflection of perfect health, let go of any attachments to specific outcomes or perceived limitations. Trust wholeheartedly that the universe has an infinite number of ways to bring your intention to fruition, and that you are fully supported in your journey towards optimal well-being. Release any doubts, fears, or limiting beliefs, knowing that they no longer serve you and that you are capable of transcending them with ease. Embrace the limitless potential within you and the boundless possibilities available to you at every turn.

Now, imagine yourself stepping through the mirror and into this world of perfect health, feeling the boundaries between your current reality and this ideal version of yourself dissolving with each confident step. As you merge with your reflection, feel a profound sense of alignment, knowing that you are one with this vision of radiant well-being. Allow the energy of perfect health to flow through every cell of your body, awakening your innate healing abilities and restoring balance to your entire being. Feel the high vibration of wellness resonating deeply in your heart, mind, and soul, anchoring itself securely within you.

Take a moment to check in with your energy and emotions, noticing any shifts or expansions in your awareness. If you encounter any negative or limiting beliefs arising, simply acknowledge them with compassion and let them pass, like clouds drifting effortlessly across the sky. Replace them with empowering thoughts and feelings that support your vision of perfect health, such as "I am worthy of vibrant health" or "My body is a self-healing miracle." Feel a deep sense of gratitude for the incredible healing capacity of your body and mind, and for the opportunity to create your reality through your intentions and beliefs.

As you prepare to return to your everyday life, carry with you the feelings of empowerment, alignment, and gratitude that you've cultivated during this transformative visualization. Know that by consistently focusing on your intention and embodying the vibration of perfect health, you are actively shaping your reality and attracting experiences that support your well-being. Express sincere appreciation for the journey you are on and trust that the universe is conspiring in your favor, bringing you the resources, opportunities, and synchronicities that will help you manifest your vision of optimal health with grace and ease.

Gently bring your awareness back to the present moment, taking a deep breath and slowly opening your eyes. As you reorient yourself to your surroundings, remember that the power to create your desired reality lies within you, and that you have the innate ability to manifest perfect health in every moment. By aligning your thoughts, emotions, and actions with your intention of vibrant well-being, you are well on your way to creating a life filled with vitality, joy, and boundless energy.

Thank you for dedicating this precious time to your personal growth and well-being. Trust completely in the power of your intentions and the infinite wisdom of the universe, knowing that you are fully supported and guided every step of the way on your journey towards perfect health. Embrace the incredible being that you are and the magnificent life that awaits you, filled with joy, abundance, and limitless potential. Remember, your reality is a reflection of your inner world, and by nourishing your mind, body, and soul with love, compassion, and positive intentions, you create a life of profound well-being and happiness. Carry this truth with you always, and watch in awe as your world transforms in miraculous ways.

16. Cultivating Freedom

Welcome to this transformative visualization session, where we will harness the power of the Reality Transurfing Mirror technique to manifest freedom. This may be financial freedom, time freedom, location freedom or all the freedoms. As we begin, set a clear intention to open your mind to the limitless possibilities that await you as you align yourself with the principles of Reality Transurfing. Embrace the idea that you have the power to shape your reality according to your desires.

Find a quiet, comfortable space where you can sit or lie down without disturbance. If you feel comfortable, close your eyes. Allow your body to settle into a state of deep relaxation, releasing any tension or tightness in your muscles. Take a slow, deep breath in through your nose, filling your lungs with fresh, cleansing air. Hold it for a moment, and then exhale slowly through your mouth, letting go of any stress, worries, or distractions. Continue this breathing pattern, focusing on the gentle rise and fall of your chest, as you cultivate a profound sense of inner calm and receptivity. With each breath, feel yourself sinking deeper into relaxation, letting go of any resistance or limitations.

As you relax, bring your attention to your intentions for this visualization. What does freedom truly mean to you? Envision yourself living a life of boundless financial abundance, where money flows effortlessly and abundantly to you, enabling you to pursue your passions, support your desired lifestyle, and make a positive impact in the world. Picture yourself having complete autonomy over your time, free to allocate it according to your priorities, values, and the activities that bring you the greatest joy and fulfillment. Imagine the freedom to choose your location, whether it's traveling to exotic destinations, living in your dream home, or creating a sanctuary that nourishes your soul and inspires your creativity. The more vividly and precisely you can define your intentions, the more effectively you'll attract them into your reality.

Now, imagine yourself standing in front of a large, ornate mirror. This is no ordinary mirror; it is the Mirror of your Reality, a powerful tool in the Reality Transurfing technique. As you gaze into the mirror, observe your reflection transforming into the version of yourself that embodies the freedom you seek. Notice every detail of this reflection – the confident posture, the radiant smile, the eyes that sparkle with joy, vitality, and fulfillment. See yourself dressed in clothing that reflects your success and abundance, surroundings that represent your ideal lifestyle. Engage all your senses as you explore this reflection, feeling the textures, hearing the sounds, and even smelling the scents associated with your desired reality. By focusing on your desired outcomes with vivid sensory detail, you attract them into your life with greater ease and speed.

As you immerse yourself in the reflection, allow yourself to feel the emotions associated with living in this state of freedom. Experience the profound joy, peace, and fulfillment that comes with living life on your own terms. Notice how your body feels – energized, vibrant, and alive, free from stress and limitations. Observe the abundance that surrounds you – the financial resources, the supportive relationships, and the opportunities that align with your deepest desires. The more intensely and authentically you can feel these positive emotions, the more powerfully you'll attract your desired reality.

Now, take a step forward and merge with your reflection in the mirror. Feel yourself becoming one with this version of yourself that lives in complete freedom. As you embody this state, notice how your energy shifts, becoming lighter, more vibrant, and aligned with your true essence. Feel the boundaries between your current reality and your desired reality dissolving, as you recognize that everything you seek already exists within you.

As you stand in this space of freedom, practice the art of letting go. Release any attachment to specific outcomes or limitations, trusting that the universe has a perfect plan for you. Surrender control and allow yourself to flow with the natural current of reality, knowing that your intentions are being woven into the fabric of your existence. If any doubts, fears, or limiting beliefs arise, acknowledge them with compassion, and then gently release them, replacing them with empowering thoughts and feelings. Affirm to yourself that you are worthy and deserving of the freedom you seek and that it is your birthright to live a life of abundance, joy, and fulfillment.

In Reality Transurfing, there is a concept known as the Alternatives Space, a realm of infinite possibilities where all potential realities exist. Imagine yourself connecting with this Alternatives Space, aligning yourself with the version of reality that resonates most strongly with your intentions for freedom. Feel the energy of your desired reality flowing through you, guiding you towards the most favorable outcomes and experiences. Trust that by aligning with the Alternatives Space, you are effortlessly navigating towards your ideal reality, as if being carried by a swift and steady current.

As you continue to embody the state of freedom, take a moment to express heartfelt gratitude for the abundance, opportunities, and experiences that are already present in your life. Acknowledge the people, resources, and circumstances that have supported you on your journey thus far. Cultivate a deep sense of appreciation for the lessons, growth, and blessings that have shaped you into the person you are today. Feel the warm, expansive energy of gratitude filling your entire being, knowing that by appreciating what you have, you open yourself to receiving even more.

Now, it's time to step back from the Mirror of your reality, knowing that you have successfully imprinted your intention for freedom onto the fabric of your existence. Take a moment to integrate the insights, emotions, and experiences you've gained from this powerful visualization. Allow the feelings of empowerment, abundance, and freedom to permeate every cell of your being, anchoring them deeply into your subconscious mind. Know that you can return to this Mirror anytime you wish to reinforce your intentions and align yourself with your desired reality.

As we prepare to conclude this visualization, take a few deep breaths, and gently bring your awareness back to the present moment. Wiggle your fingers and toes, feeling the connection between your body and the surface beneath you. When you're ready, slowly open your eyes, feeling refreshed, energized, and aligned with your path to ultimate freedom.

Carry the insights and energy from this visualization with you as you move forward in your daily life. Trust in the principles of Reality Transurfing, stay true to your intentions, and embrace the journey with an open heart and mind. Remember that the power to create your desired reality lies within you and that by aligning your thoughts, emotions, and actions with your intentions, you become an unstoppable force in manifesting your dreams.

May your path be filled with abundant financial resources, the freedom to control your time, and the ability to choose your location based on your heart's desires. Embrace the limitless possibilities that await you as you navigate the incredible journey of life, knowing that the universe is conspiring in your favor, guiding you towards the highest expression of your potential.

PRACTICE REALITY TRANSURFING

Embrace your role as the creator of your reality and know that by aligning with the principles of Reality Transurfing, you have the power to shape your life in extraordinary ways. May your journey be filled with joy, abundance, and the ultimate freedom to live life on your own terms. Thank you for your presence and commitment to your growth. Enjoy the limitless possibilities that await you!

17. Manifesting a Life of Ease and Flow

To embark on this transformative journey, begin by finding a peaceful, comfortable space where you can relax without any interruptions or distractions. Ensure that you are wearing loose, comfortable clothing and that the temperature of the room is set to a level that promotes relaxation.

Once you have found a suitable position, either sitting or lying down, gently close your eyes and take a few slow, deep breaths. As you inhale, fill your lungs with fresh, rejuvenating air, and as you exhale, release any tension, stress, or worries that may be lingering in your body or mind. With each successive breath, allow yourself to sink deeper into a state of profound relaxation, cultivating a deep sense of inner calm, tranquility, and receptivity.

Now, bring your focus to your intention for this visualization – manifesting a life filled with ease, flow, and effortless unfolding. Envision yourself navigating through challenges and obstacles with grace and ease, as if you are dancing through life with a sense of lightness and fluidity. Picture opportunities and resources flowing to you with perfect timing and alignment, as if the universe is conspiring to support your every desire and aspiration. Imagine yourself radiating an energy of calm confidence, trusting implicitly in the unwavering support and guidance of the universe. Take a moment to define this vision as clearly and vividly as possible, engaging all of your senses to make the experience more real, tangible, and immersive.

Next, imagine yourself standing before a large, ornate mirror – the Mirror of your Reality. As you gaze into the mirror, observe your reflection gradually transforming into the version of yourself that embodies the ease and flow you seek. Notice the serene and peaceful expression on your face, the relaxed and open posture, and the eyes that sparkle with trust, contentment, and inner knowing. See yourself moving through life with effortless grace, surrounded by beauty, abundance, and the perfect unfolding of your deepest desires and aspirations. Engage all of your senses as you explore this reflection – feel the gentle touch of tranquility on your skin, hear the soothing sounds of harmony and balance, and immerse yourself in the scents of your desired reality.

As you continue to observe your reflection, allow yourself to deeply feel the emotions associated with living a life of ease and flow. Experience the profound serenity, joy, and fulfillment that comes from being in perfect alignment with your true path and purpose. Notice how your body feels – relaxed, energized, and free from any tension, pain, or struggle. Observe the effortless unfolding of your day, the perfect synchronicities that guide you, and the abundant resources and supportive relationships that surround you. Take your time to fully immerse yourself in these positive emotions, allowing them to become rich, vivid, authentic, and deeply ingrained in your being.

When you feel ready, take a step forward and merge with your reflection in the mirror, becoming one with this version of yourself that lives with absolute ease and flow. As you embody this state, notice how your energy shifts, becoming lighter, more vibrant, and resonating with your deepest truth, purpose, and potential. Feel the boundaries dissolving between your current reality and your desired reality, recognizing that everything you seek already exists within you, waiting to be awakened, expressed, and manifested.

In this space of ease and flow, practice the art of letting go and surrendering. Release any attachment to specific outcomes, timelines, or expectations, trusting fully in the universe's perfect plan and timing for you. Surrender control and allow yourself to flow with the natural current of reality, knowing that your intentions are being woven into the very fabric of your existence, guiding you towards your highest good. If any doubts, fears, or limiting beliefs arise, acknowledge them with compassion and understanding, then gently release them, replacing them with empowering thoughts, feelings, and affirmations that support your vision and align with your true essence.

Now, imagine yourself connecting with the Alternatives Space – a realm of infinite potential where all possible realities exist simultaneously. Feel yourself aligning with the version of reality that most strongly resonates with your intentions for ease, flow, and graceful unfolding. Allow the energy of your desired reality to flow through you, guiding you towards the most favorable outcomes, experiences, and opportunities. Realize that as you do this, you are being gently carried by a swift and steady current towards your ultimate destination and the fulfillment of your deepest desires.

As you continue embodying the state of ease and flow, take a moment to express heartfelt gratitude for the grace, synchronicity, and blessings that are already present in your life. Acknowledge the people, resources, experiences, and lessons that have supported you on your journey thus far, recognizing the invaluable role they have played in your growth, evolution, and transformation. Feel the warm, expansive energy of gratitude filling your entire being, knowing that by appreciating what you have, you open yourself to receiving even more abundance, joy, love, and fulfillment in all areas of your life.

When you feel ready, step back from the Mirror of your reality, knowing that you have successfully imprinted your intention for a life of ease and flow onto the fabric of your existence, setting in motion a powerful chain of events that will manifest your desires with effortless grace. Take a few deep, cleansing breaths and gently bring your awareness back to the present moment, grounding yourself in the here and now. Wiggle your fingers and toes, feeling the connection between your body and the surface beneath you, anchoring yourself in the physical reality while maintaining the energetic connection to your desired state of being.

Slowly open your eyes, feeling refreshed, energized, and fully aligned with your path of ease and flow. Carry the insights, energy, and transformation from this visualization with you as you move forward in your daily life, allowing them to guide, inspire, and uplift you. Trust in the principles of Reality Transurfing, stay true to your intentions, and embrace the journey with an open heart, a curious mind, and a deep sense of faith and knowing.

Remember, you have the innate power to shape your reality in extraordinary and miraculous ways, co-creating a life that exceeds your wildest dreams and expectations. By aligning your thoughts, emotions, and actions with your intentions, you become an unstoppable force in manifesting your heart's desires and living a life of profound purpose, meaning, and fulfillment. May your path be filled with graceful unfolding, perfect synchronicity, and an unwavering sense of ease and flow, as you navigate the incredible journey of life with wisdom, courage, and an open, loving heart. Embrace the limitless possibilities that await you, knowing that the universe conspires in your favor, guiding you towards your highest potential, the fullest expression of your being, and the creation of a reality that reflects your deepest desires and aspirations.

May this visualization serve as a powerful catalyst for your transformation, empowering you to live a life of ease, flow, and abundant blessings, as you continue to grow, evolve, and expand in consciousness, love, and light. Trust in the journey, trust in yourself, and trust in the unwavering support of the universe, as you navigate the path of your highest destiny with grace, courage, and an open, grateful heart.

18. Manifesting Miracles and Synchronicities

Welcome to this transformative visualization session, where we will harness the power of the Reality Transurfing Mirror technique to manifest miracles and synchronicities in your daily life. As we begin, set a clear intention to open your mind to the extraordinary possibilities that await you as you align yourself with the principles of Reality Transurfing. Embrace the idea that you have the power to co-create your reality with the universe, attracting magical experiences and meaningful coincidences.

Find a quiet, comfortable space where you can sit or lie down without disturbance. When you feel comfortable, close your eyes. Allow your body to settle into a state of deep relaxation, releasing any tension or tightness in your muscles. Take a slow, deep breath in through your nose, filling your lungs with fresh, cleansing air. Hold it for a moment, and then exhale slowly through your mouth, letting go of any stress, worries, or distractions. Continue this breathing pattern, focusing on the gentle rise and fall of your chest, as you cultivate a profound sense of inner calm and receptivity. With each breath, feel yourself sinking deeper into relaxation, letting go of any resistance or limitations.

As you relax, bring your attention to your intentions for this visualization. What does experiencing miracles and synchronicities in your daily life mean to you? Envision yourself moving through your day with a heightened sense of awareness, noticing the subtle yet profound signs, messages, and opportunities that the universe presents to you. Picture yourself encountering serendipitous events that align perfectly with your desires and intentions, as if the universe is conspiring in your favor. Imagine meeting the right people at the right time, discovering hidden treasures and insights, and experiencing a deep sense of connection and purpose in every moment. The more vividly and precisely you can define your intentions, the more effectively you'll attract these experiences into your reality.

Now, imagine yourself standing in front of a large, elaborate mirror. This is no ordinary mirror; it is the Mirror of your Reality, a powerful tool in the Reality Transurfing technique. As you gaze into the mirror, observe your reflection transforming into the version of yourself that embodies a life filled with miracles and synchronicities. Notice every detail of this reflection – the radiant glow emanating from your being. See the sparkle in your eyes that reflects your innate wisdom and connection to the divine. Embrace the serene smile that expresses your trust in the unfolding of your journey. See yourself moving through your day with grace, ease, and a profound sense of wonder, as the universe reveals its magic to you in countless ways. Engage all your senses as you explore this reflection, feeling the tingling sensations of excitement and anticipation, hearing the whispers of guidance and inspiration, and even smelling the sweet fragrance of divine presence that surrounds you. By focusing on your desired outcomes with vivid sensory detail, you attract them into your life with greater ease and speed.

As you immerse yourself in the reflection, allow yourself to feel the emotions associated with living a life filled with miracles and synchronicities. Experience the profound joy, gratitude, and awe that comes with recognizing the universe's loving support and guidance in every moment. Notice how your body feels – light, energized, and attuned to the subtle frequencies of the cosmos. Observe the synchronicities that unfold before you – the perfect timing of events, the unexpected blessings, and the divine interventions that guide you towards your highest path. The more intensely and authentically you can feel these positive emotions, the more powerfully you'll attract your desired reality.

Now, take a step forward and merge with your reflection in the mirror. Feel yourself becoming one with this version of yourself that lives in a constant state of miraculous unfolding and synchronicity. As you embody this state, notice how your energy shifts, becoming more vibrant, harmonious, and aligned with the universal flow. Feel the boundaries between the ordinary and the extraordinary dissolving, as you recognize that miracles are your birthright, and that the universe is always communicating with you through signs and synchronicities.

As you stand in this space of divine connection, practice the art of surrender. Release any attachment to specific outcomes or expectations, trusting that the universe has a perfect plan for you. Let go of the need to control or force things to happen, and instead, allow yourself to be guided by the gentle whispers of your intuition and the loving hand of the divine. If any doubts, fears, or limiting beliefs arise, acknowledge them with compassion, and then gently release them, replacing them with faith, trust, and a deep knowing that you are always supported and loved. Affirm to yourself that you are a magnet for miracles and that synchronicities are the language of the universe, guiding you towards your highest good.

In Reality Transurfing, there is a concept known as the Alternatives Space. This is a realm of infinite possibilities where all potential realities exist. Imagine yourself connecting with this Alternatives Space, aligning yourself with the versions of reality that resonate most strongly with your intentions for a life filled with miracles and synchronicities. Feel the energy of your desired reality flowing through you, guiding you towards the most magical and meaningful experiences. Trust that by aligning with the Alternatives Space, you are effortlessly navigating towards a life of divine unfolding, where every step is guided by the loving hand of the universe.

As you continue to embody the state of miraculous living, take a moment to express heartfelt gratitude for the blessings, opportunities, and synchronicities that are already present in your life. Acknowledge the people, experiences, and insights that have served as divine messengers, guiding you towards your highest path. Cultivate a deep sense of appreciation for the mystery and magic of existence, knowing that by embracing gratitude, you open yourself to receiving even more miracles and blessings. Feel the warm, expansive energy of gratitude filling your entire being, knowing that by appreciating the miracles in your life, you attract even more miraculous experiences.

Now, it's time to step back from the Mirror of your reality, knowing that you have successfully imprinted your intention for a life filled with miracles and synchronicities onto the fabric of your existence. Take a moment to integrate the insights, emotions, and experiences you've gained from this powerful visualization. Allow the feelings of wonder, divine connection, and trust to permeate every cell of your being, anchoring them deeply into your subconscious mind. Know that you can return to this Mirror anytime you wish to reinforce your intentions and align yourself with the magic of the universe.

As we prepare to conclude this visualization, take a few deep breaths, and gently bring your awareness back to the present moment. Wiggle your fingers and toes, feeling the connection between your body and the surface beneath you. When you're ready, slowly open your eyes, feeling refreshed, energized, and aligned with the miraculous flow of the universe.

Carry the insights and energy from this visualization with you as you move forward in your daily life. Trust in the principles of Reality Transurfing, stay open to the signs and synchronicities that guide you, and embrace the journey with a sense of wonder and curiosity. Remember that you are always supported by the loving presence of the universe and that miracles are unfolding in every moment, waiting for you to recognize and embrace them.

May your path be filled with countless miracles, profound synchronicities, and a deep sense of trust in the unfolding of your journey. Embrace your role as a co-creator with the universe, knowing that by aligning your thoughts, emotions, and actions with your highest intentions, you invite the most extraordinary experiences into your life.

May your journey be filled with the magic and wonder of a life lived in harmony with the divine. Trust in the miracles that await you and know that the universe is always conspiring in your favor, guiding you towards the most beautiful and meaningful experiences. Thank you for your presence and commitment to your spiritual growth. Enjoy the miraculous unfolding of your path!

19. Discovering Your Life Purpose

Welcome to this transformative journey of uncovering your life purpose through the power of Reality Transurfing. As we begin this visualization, take a moment to set a clear intention for the insight and clarity you wish to gain about your true calling. Perhaps you long to understand how your unique gifts and passions can be of service to the world, or maybe you seek a deeper sense of meaning and fulfillment in your life path. Whatever your intention may be, trust that through the principles of Reality Transurfing, you have the power to access the wisdom within and align with your highest purpose. Reality Transurfing teaches us that our outer reality is a reflection of our inner state, and by consciously focusing our thoughts and energy on our goals, we become the creators of our own destiny.

Find a quiet space where you can be free from distractions and allow yourself to fully relax. Settle into a comfortable position, whether seated or lying down, and begin to bring your attention to your breath. Inhale deeply, filling your lungs with fresh, cleansing air, and exhale slowly, releasing any tension or stress that you may be holding in your body. With each breath, feel yourself sinking deeper into a state of peace and tranquility, letting go of any worries or thoughts that may be clouding your mind. Allow your breath to be your anchor, guiding you into a profound state of inner stillness. As you continue to breathe deeply, notice how your body becomes heavier, melting into the surface beneath you. Feel the gentle rise and fall of your chest, the rhythmic flow of air in and out of your nostrils, and the gradual quieting of your mind. In this state of deep relaxation, you become more receptive to the wisdom and guidance within

Now, bring your focus to your intention for discovering your life purpose. Take a moment to connect with the deepest part of yourself, the part that holds the key to your true calling. Perhaps you feel a gentle stirring in your heart, a whisper of your soul guiding you towards your higher path. Trust in this inner knowing and allow yourself to explore what truly lights you up and brings you a sense of fulfillment. As you hold this intention in your mind, affirm to yourself, "I am open to receiving clarity and guidance about my life purpose. I trust in the wisdom of my soul to lead me towards my highest path." Feel the power of your words resonating through every cell of your being, anchoring your intention into your reality.

As you continue to hold your intention, imagine yourself transported to a beautiful, serene space. This could be a majestic mountain top overlooking a vast landscape, a tranquil forest filled with ancient trees, or any other location that evokes a sense of awe and wonder within you. In this sacred space, you encounter a large, golden mirror. As you approach the mirror, you see your reflection transforming into your highest, most authentic self. You radiate an energy of pure love, wisdom, and purpose. The mirror reflects back to you the truth of who you are and the unique gifts you have to offer the world.

Visualize yourself stepping into the mirror, merging with your highest self. As you do so, feel a profound sense of alignment and clarity washing over you. In this space, you have access to the deepest wisdom of your soul, and you can ask for guidance about your life purpose. Notice any images, symbols, or insights that arise in your mind's eye. Perhaps you see yourself engaging in activities that bring you joy and fulfillment, or you receive a clear message about the impact you are meant to make in the world. Allow these insights to flow to you effortlessly, trusting that they hold the key to your true calling.

As you receive these visions and messages, engage all your senses to make the experience more vivid and real. Notice the colors, sounds, textures, and feelings associated with your life purpose. The more fully you immerse yourself in this experience, the more deeply it becomes imprinted in your subconscious mind, paving the way for its manifestation in your reality. Remember, the mirror is a powerful tool, reflecting back to you the truth of your innermost being. As you focus on your highest purpose, the mirror will continue to reflect that clarity and alignment.

As you bask in the clarity and wisdom of your highest self, take a moment to release any attachment to specific outcomes or timelines. Recognize that your life purpose is a journey, not a destination, and that it may unfold in ways you cannot yet imagine. Surrender any need to control or force the process, and instead, embrace a deep sense of trust in the universe's plan for you. Know that as you continue to align your thoughts, actions, and energy with your true calling, the path will be revealed to you step by step. Release any doubts or fears, knowing that the more you let go, the more space you create for miracles to occur in your life.

In this state of surrender, allow yourself to connect with the Alternatives Space, the realm of infinite possibilities that exists beyond the limitations of your current reality. In this space, you have access to the version of reality where your life purpose is already being lived out in its fullest expression. Feel yourself merging with the energy of this Alternatives Space, where joy, fulfillment, and alignment are the natural order. Allow the wisdom of your heart to guide you, trusting that you are always being supported and directed towards your highest good. In this space, there are no obstacles or barriers, only endless potential for growth and transformation. Embrace the knowing that as you align with the Alternatives Space, your life in the physical world will begin to mirror the clarity and purpose you experience here.

As you continue to bask in the energy of the Alternatives Space, take a moment to check in with your own energy and emotions. Notice any areas where you may be holding onto limiting beliefs or fears that are blocking you from fully embracing your life purpose. Perhaps there are old stories or doubts that need to be acknowledged and released. Take a deep breath and imagine these limiting beliefs being gently dissolved by the light of your awareness. As you exhale, feel them leaving your body and dissipating into the ether. Replace these old patterns with empowering beliefs such as, "I am worthy of living a life filled with purpose and meaning," "I trust in the unfolding of my journey," and "I am capable of making a positive impact in the world." Feel your energy shifting, becoming lighter, clearer, and more aligned with your highest truth.

In this space of clarity and alignment, allow a profound sense of gratitude to wash over you. Give thanks for the unique gifts and talents that you have been blessed with, and for the opportunities that have led you to this moment of insight and understanding. Recognize that every experience in your life, whether joyful or challenging, has been a stepping stone towards your highest purpose. Appreciate the lessons you've learned, the growth you've experienced, and the wisdom you've gained along the way. Gratitude is a powerful magnet, attracting more of what you appreciate into your life. The more you focus on the blessings and opportunities in your life, the more reasons you'll find to be grateful.

As you prepare to return to your waking reality, take a moment to integrate the insights and experiences you've had during this visualization. Allow the feelings of clarity, purpose, and empowerment to anchor themselves deeply into your being. Know that you have the power to live a life filled with meaning and fulfillment by aligning your thoughts, words, and actions with the truth of your highest self. Carry the energy of this visualization with you as you navigate your daily life, remembering that you are the creator of your reality. Trust that the seeds of insight planted in this sacred space will blossom in perfect timing, guiding you towards your true calling.

Gently begin to bring your awareness back to your physical body, wiggling your fingers and toes, and taking a deep, cleansing breath. Feel the energy of the room around you, the surface beneath you, and the gentle rhythm of your breath. When you're ready, slowly open your eyes, feeling refreshed, centered, and filled with a renewed sense of purpose and direction.

Thank you for dedicating this time to uncovering your life purpose and creating a reality filled with meaning, fulfillment, and alignment. Trust in the journey and have faith that the universe is conspiring in your favor, bringing you the perfect experiences and opportunities to support your highest path. Remember that your purpose is not something to be found, but rather something to be created and expressed through the unique lens of your being. Embrace the adventure of discovering and living out your true calling, knowing that the world needs the gifts that only you can offer.

.

20. Achieving a State of Emotional Mastery and Resilience

Welcome to this transformative visualization session where we will harness the power of Reality Transurfing to cultivate emotional mastery. As we embark on this journey together, let us set a clear and purposeful intention to align our emotional well-being with the natural flow of the universe. By doing so, we open ourselves to the infinite possibilities available to us, allowing our desired state of inner peace and strength to manifest with effortless grace. Reality Transurfing teaches us that our thoughts and beliefs hold the power to shape our reality. By consciously choosing and focusing on our intentions, we become the architects of our own emotional landscape. The Principle of Intention reminds us that our minded focus and unwavering determination have the ability to bring forth the reality we desire.

To begin, find a comfortable position, either seated or lying down, and allow your eyes to gently close. Take a deep, cleansing breath, inhaling tranquility and exhaling any tensions or worries that may have accumulated throughout your day. As you continue to breathe slowly and deliberately, feel your body sinking into a state of deep relaxation. With each exhale, imagine any remaining stress or emotional turbulence melting away, leaving you feeling centered and at peace. Embrace this sensation of inner calm, knowing that in this space of serenity, you are most receptive to the transformative power of this visualization.

Now, bring your attention to the intentions you hold for this visualization and your emotional journey as a whole. Take a moment to contemplate what it is you truly wish to achieve. Visualize yourself as the embodiment of emotional mastery and resilience, radiating balance, adaptability, and unwavering strength. See yourself navigating life's challenges with grace and poise, responding to adversity with wisdom and compassion. Affirm to yourself, "I am the creator of my emotional well-being. I deal with life's challenges in a knowing and calm manner." Feel the resonance of this statement echoing through every cell of your being, aligning your desires with your intentions. Trust in your innate ability to manifest your chosen reality of emotional harmony and resilience.

Allow your imagination to transport you to a serene and nurturing inner sanctuary, a space designed to support your emotional growth and development. As you settle into this space, imagine a magnificent mirror standing before you, its surface reflecting the infinite potential within you. This mirror represents the Reality Transurfing Mirror Technique, a powerful tool for aligning your inner world with your desired external reality. Gaze deeply into the mirror, and see your reflection as the embodiment of emotional mastery and resilience. Notice the unwavering strength and adaptability in your eyes, the grace and poise in your posture. As you continue to observe your reflection, feel a profound sense of connection and unity with your highest potential. Allow yourself to absorb the qualities of emotional balance, flexibility, and endurance, knowing that these attributes reside within you, waiting to be fully expressed.

As you hold this empowering vision in your mind's eye, take a moment to release any attachment to specific outcomes or self-imposed limitations. Acknowledge that the path to emotional mastery is a continuous journey of growth and self-discovery, and that is okay. Trust in the infinite wisdom of the universe to guide you towards your desired state of being in the most harmonious and beneficial way possible. Surrender any need for control, knowing that by aligning your intentions with the natural flow of life, you open yourself to a world of profound inner peace and resilience. Embrace the flow of your emotions, recognizing that each experience, whether joyful or challenging, is an essential part of your unique path to emotional mastery.

Now, let us connect with the transformative concept of the Alternatives Space, a dimension beyond our everyday reality where all potentials exist simultaneously. Imagine yourself tapping into this infinite realm, aligning with the version of reality that fully supports and nurtures your emotional well-being. Feel the boundless energy of this space flowing through you, infusing every cell of your being with the unwavering belief in your ability to achieve emotional harmony and resilience. Visualize yourself effortlessly attracting the resources, opportunities, and support necessary for your emotional growth. See doors of possibility swinging open before you, revealing exciting new avenues for self-discovery and inner transformation. Trust that in this Alternatives Space, your intentions for emotional mastery are fully supported and manifested with ease and grace. The principle of the Alternatives Space enables us to expand our perception beyond the limitations of our current emotional state, recognizing that we have the power to align with the most favorable outcomes available to us.

As you continue to immerse yourself in this empowering visualization, return your focus to the mirror before you. Notice any negative or limiting beliefs that may be lingering in the depths of your mind, quietly undermining your emotional well-being. Acknowledge these thoughts without judgment, understanding that they are simply old patterns that no longer serve you. With a gentle exhale, release these limiting beliefs, watching them dissolve from your reflection in the mirror. In their place, see the reflection of your empowered self, radiating positive affirmations and beliefs. Repeat to yourself, "I am capable of achieving emotional mastery and resilience. I trust in my innate ability to navigate life's challenges with grace and wisdom." Feel the vibrational resonance of these statements infusing every aspect of your being, from the tiniest atom to the vast expanses of your consciousness. Allow these affirmations to take root, blossoming into an unshakable faith in your own emotional strength and adaptability. By consciously choosing to focus on uplifting thoughts and beliefs, you attract experiences and circumstances that reflect your positive inner state.

As you bask in the glow of your own transformative power, take a moment to cultivate a profound sense of gratitude for the abundance of opportunities for emotional growth and resilience in your life. Recognize that each challenge you encounter along your journey is a precious gift, offering you the chance to develop greater self-awareness, compassion, and inner strength. Embrace the full spectrum of your emotions with a heart full of appreciation, knowing that every experience, no matter how difficult, is guiding you towards a state of profound emotional mastery. Give thanks for the wisdom gained from past experiences, the support of loved ones, and the boundless strength that resides within you. Allow this gratitude to fill your entire being, radiating outward and attracting even more blessings into your life. As you maintain a constant state of appreciation, you open yourself to the limitless abundance of the universe.

As we prepare to release this visualization, take a final moment to integrate the profound insights and transformative experiences you have gained. Acknowledge the shifts in your perspective, the newfound clarity of your intentions, and the unshakable confidence in your ability to manifest emotional mastery and resilience. Embrace the feelings of empowerment and alignment, knowing that they will continue to guide and support you long after this visualization has ended. Visualize yourself carrying this radiant energy with you as you navigate your daily life, infusing your interactions and experiences with the vibrant essence of your highest potential. Trust in the unwavering support of the universe, knowing that your emotional journey is unfolding in perfect harmony with your deepest desires.

As you slowly begin to bring your awareness back to the present moment, take a deep, cleansing breath, feeling the gentle rise and fall of your chest. Wiggle your fingers and toes, gradually reawakening your physical senses. When you feel ready, gently open your eyes, allowing them to adjust to the light around you. Carry the peaceful energy and unwavering intention of this visualization with you as you continue on your path to emotional mastery and resilience. Remember that your dedication to personal growth and your alignment with the principles of Reality Transurfing will continue to manifest profound well-being and strength in your external reality.

21. Achieving a State of Optimal Mental Clarity

Begin by finding a quiet, comfortable space where you can be undisturbed. Take a moment to set a clear, powerful intention for this practice - to cultivate a state of deep, unshakable mental clarity and laser-like focus that will profoundly elevate your productivity, decision-making, and overall well-being. Really connect with the transformative power of this intention, knowing that by consciously choosing to align your mind with crystalline clarity and unwavering focus, you are actively shaping your reality in the most positive and profound ways.

Settle into a relaxed position, either seated or lying down, and gently close your eyes. Bring your full attention to your breath, observing the natural, rhythmic ebb and flow of air moving in and out of your body. Inhale deeply, feeling your lungs expand fully, and then exhale slowly, mindfully releasing any tension, stress, or mental chatter you may be holding onto. Continue this deep, conscious breathing, allowing each breath to guide you into an ever deeper state of relaxation, tranquility and inner stillness. If any thoughts arise, simply witness them without attachment or judgment, and gently return your focus to your breath, to the present moment. Allow yourself to sink into the profound peace and stillness that always resides within you, that is your natural state of being.

Now, begin to visualize yourself in an extraordinarily serene, beautiful, and expansive space that evokes a sense of deep peace, spaciousness and clarity. This could be a magnificent crystal cave with soaring, luminous walls, a tranquil, light-filled meditation room, or a lush, fragrant garden with soothing fountains and abundant, vibrant flora. Use all of your senses to make this visualization as vivid, immersive and real as possible. Feel the gentle, refreshing air on your skin, hear the calming, soothing sounds of your surroundings, and breathe in the energizing, clarifying, and purifying atmosphere. Fully allow yourself to arrive in this sanctuary of clarity and focus, to feel at home here.

As you explore this peaceful inner landscape, you notice a magnificent, ornate mirror standing before you, beckoning to you. The mirror is framed in gleaming, radiant gold, and its surface is perfectly clear, smooth and still, like a pristine, tranquil lake on a windless day. You approach the mirror, feeling a growing sense of reverence, anticipation, and joyful excitement, knowing deep within that this is an immensely powerful tool for transformation, self-realization, and the activation of your highest potential.

Standing before the mirror now, gaze deeply into its luminous, reflective surface. As you look, observe your reflection begin to shift and change, revealing and unveiling the version of yourself with the most crystalline, diamond-like mental clarity and laser-like, unwavering focus you can possibly imagine. Take in how radiant, luminous and magnetic you appear, your eyes sparkling with the light of pure intelligence, insight, and profound wisdom, your entire being emanating an aura of deep knowing, understanding, and unshakable presence. Notice the way you carry yourself - grounded, centered, and fully anchored in the present moment, in your power. The mirror reflects back to you the image of your optimal mental state, affirming it as your true, unbounded essence and your limitless birthright.

As you absorb this empowering, inspiring reflection, silently and powerfully affirm to yourself: "I am now fully aligned with my highest state of mental clarity and focus. My mind is sharp, clear, expansive and fully present. I now release any and all thoughts or patterns that do not serve my highest good and my most luminous self, and wholeheartedly embrace the liberating truth of my limitless potential." Feel these affirmations resonating through every cell of your being, reprogramming your subconscious mind and aligning you with your optimal, illuminated state.

Now, imagine yourself boldly stepping through the mirror, merging fully with your reflection of optimal mental clarity and focus, uniting with this highest version of yourself. As you do so, feel a profound, unmistakable shift occurring within you - a deep, unshakable sense of inner stillness, clarity, and absolutely certain knowing. Allow this feeling to permeate and saturate your entire being, filling you with a sense of profound mental acuity, diamond-like clarity, and unwavering, laser-like focus.

In this merged, unified state, you find yourself effortlessly stepping into the Alternative Space - the realm of infinite possibilities where your optimal mental state already exists in its fullest, most radiant expression. Here, in this space, there are no limitations, obstacles or barriers, only the endless, boundless potential for insight, understanding, growth and expansion. Feel yourself embodying the qualities of crystal clarity and laser-like focus, navigating through this luminous space with effortless ease, grace and flow. Observe how your thoughts seamlessly flow with precision, purpose and power, how your intuition guides you effortlessly towards your highest choices and actions, and how you approach challenges and opportunities with a sense of calm, centered confidence and unshakable trust. Allow yourself to fully embrace, embody and radiate this elevated, luminous state of being.

As you continue to explore the Alternative Space, take a moment to cultivate a deep, heartfelt sense of gratitude for your remarkable mind, for your consciousness, and its truly boundless capacities. Give thanks for your innate ability to access and sustain profound states of clarity, focus, and insight, and for the myriad blessings, opportunities and shifts that this optimal mental state will manifest and magnify in your life. Feel

113 | PRACTICE REALITY TRANSURFING

deep appreciation for the entire journey that has brought you to this point, recognizing that every experience, every challenge, has served to refine, strengthen and illuminate your mind, your being. Allow this gratitude to fill your heart, to fill your entire being, anchoring your intentions and powerfully magnetizing your desired reality.

When you feel ready, begin to visualize yourself gracefully stepping back through the mirror, bringing the qualities, energies and knowing of your optimal mental state with you. As you merge back into your physical body, powerfully affirm to yourself: "I now carry the clarity, focus, and profound wisdom of my highest self with me in every moment, in every breath. These qualities are an absolutely integral, unshakable part of my being, and I express them effortlessly, joyfully and radiantly in all that I do, in all that I am."

Take a deep, cleansing breath, filling your being with light, wiggle your fingers and toes, feeling your deep connection to your physical self, and gently open your eyes. As you reorient to your surroundings, to the physical world, know with unshakable certainty that the profound mental clarity and unwavering focus you experienced in the Alternative Space are now fully integrated into your being, forever available to you whenever you need them, whenever you call upon them. Carry this inner stillness, this lucidity, this presence with you as you move through your day, trusting completely in your innate wisdom and your unlimited capacity to navigate life with grace, with purpose, with profound ease and joy.

Remember, the power to achieve and sustain a state of optimal mental clarity and laser-like focus, to live from this illuminated state, is always within you. By regularly practicing this transformative Mirror Technique visualization and deeply integrating the principles of Reality Transurfing into your life, into your being, you will naturally find yourself living from this elevated state more and more of the time, until it simply becomes your natural, effortless way of being.

Embrace your innate greatness, your boundless light, and allow it to shine ever more brightly, illuminating the path ahead and guiding you, moment by moment, to a life of profound purpose, fulfillment, joy, ease and unimaginable expansion. You are ready for this, you are worthy of this, and all of life is cheering you on, now and always. Trust, shine, and enjoy the miraculous journey of remembering and embodying your truest, most radiant self.

AFTERTHOUGHT

As we come to the end of this transformative journey into the art and science of Reality Transurfing, I invite you to take a moment to reflect on the profound shifts and insights you have experienced. Through the practice of the Mirror Technique and the integration of the other principles of Reality Transurfing, you have tapped into a wellspring of wisdom, resilience, and creative power that has always resided within you.

Remember, the visualizations that you have been exposed to are not merely concepts to be understood intellectually, but rather, they are living, dynamic practices to be embodied and applied in every moment of your life. The more you engage with these practices, the more you will find yourself naturally living from a place of clarity, focus, and abundance.

As you continue on your path, there will undoubtedly be challenges, obstacles, and moments of uncertainty. In these times, trust in the power of your inner clarity and focus to guide you through. Remember that every challenge is an opportunity for growth, for expansion, and for the deepening of your connection to your authentic self.

And as you navigate the path ahead, remember that you are not alone. You are part of a global community of individuals who are awakening to their true nature and who are committed to creating a world of greater clarity, focus, wisdom, and love. By embodying these qualities in your own life, you inspire and empower others to do the same, creating a powerful ripple effect of positive change.

So go forth with clarity, with focus, and with the unshakable knowing that you are a powerful creator, capable of shaping your reality and manifesting your deepest dreams. Trust in the journey, trust in yourself, and know that the universe is conspiring in your favor, now and always.

May your path be filled with profound insights, joyful discoveries, and the ever-deepening realization of your own boundless nature. And may you always remember the simple, yet profound truth that lies at the heart of Reality Transurfing:

You are the sculptor of your own reality, and the power to create the life of your dreams lies within you, waiting to be awakened and expressed.

With deepest gratitude and boundless love,

John Bell

Printed in Dunstable, United Kingdom